1st EDITION

Perspectives on Modern World History

The 1967 Detroit Riots

1st EDITION

Perspectives on Modern World History

The 1967 Detroit Riots

Noah Berlatsky

Editor

GREENHAVEN PRESS
A part of Gale, Cengage Learning

Detroit • New York • San Francisco • New Haven, Conn • Waterville, Maine • London

Elizabeth Des Chenes, *Director, Publishing Solutions*

© 2013 Greenhaven Press, a part of Gale, Cengage Learning.

Gale and Greenhaven Press are registered trademarks used herein under license.

For more information, contact:
Greenhaven Press
27500 Drake Rd.
Farmington Hills, MI 48331-3535
Or you can visit our Internet site at gale.cengage.com.

For product information and technology assistance, contact us at
Gale Customer Support, 1-800-877-4253.

For permission to use material from this text or product, submit all requests online at
www.cengage.com/permissions.

Further permissions questions can be e-mailed to permissionrequest@cengage.com.

Articles in Greenhaven Press anthologies are often edited for length to meet page requirements. In addition, original titles of these works are changed to clearly present the main thesis and to explicitly indicate the author's opinion. Every effort is made to ensure that Greenhaven Press accurately reflects the original intent of the authors. Every effort has been made to trace the owners of copyrighted material.

Cover images © Bettmann/Corbis.

LIBRARY OF CONGRESS CATALOGING-IN-PUBLICATION DATA
The 1967 Detroit riots / Noah Berlatsky, book editor.
   p. cm. -- (Perspectives on modern world history)
   Includes bibliographical references and index.
   ISBN 978-0-7377-6362-1 (hardcover)
   1. Detroit (Mich.)--Race relations. 2. Detroit (Mich.)--History. 3. African Americans--Michigan--Detroit--History. 4. Riots--Michigan--Detroit--History. I. Berlatsky, Noah.
   F574.D49N422 2013
   305.8009774'34--dc23
                                                                   2012036908

Printed in the United States of America
1 2 3 4 5 6 7 17 16 15 14 13

CONTENTS

police and National Guard members kidnapped, killed, and brutalized civilians during the Detroit riots.

CHAPTER 2   Controversies Surrounding the 1967 Detroit Riots study race relations concludes that blacks in the United States face serious structural disadvantages. The commission argues that more government programs are needed to combat inequality.

FOREWORD

"History cannot give us a program for the future, but it can give us a fuller understanding of ourselves, and of our common humanity, so that we can better face the future."
—Robert Penn Warren,
American poet and novelist

The history of each nation is punctuated by momentous events that represent turning points for that nation, with an impact felt far beyond its borders. These events—displaying the full range of human capabilities, from violence, greed, and ignorance to heroism, courage, and strength—are nearly always complicated and multifaceted. Any student of history faces the challenge of grasping the many strands that constitute such world-changing events as wars, social movements, and environmental disasters. But understanding these significant historic events can be enhanced by exposure to a variety of perspectives, whether of people involved intimately or of ones observing from a distance of miles or years. Understanding can also be increased by learning about the controversies surrounding such events and exploring hot-button issues from multiple angles. Finally, true understanding of important historic events involves knowledge of the events' human impact—of the ways such events affected people in their everyday lives—all over the world.

Perspectives on Modern World History examines global historic events from the twentieth century onward by presenting analysis and observation from numerous vantage points. Each volume offers high school, early college level, and general interest readers a thematically arranged anthology of previously published materials that address a major historical event, with an emphasis on international coverage. Each volume opens with background information on the event, then presents the controversies surrounding that event, and concludes with first-person narratives from people who lived through the event or were affected by it. By providing primary sources from the time of the event, as well as relevant commentary surrounding the event, this series can be used to inform debate, help develop critical thinking skills, increase global awareness, and enhance an understanding of international perspectives on history.

Material in each volume is selected from a diverse range of sources, including journals, magazines, newspapers, nonfiction books, personal narratives, speeches, congressional testimony, government documents, pamphlets, organization newsletters, and position papers. Articles taken from these sources are carefully edited and introduced to provide context and background. Each volume of Perspectives on Modern World History includes an array of views on events of global significance. Much of the material comes from international sources and from US sources that provide extensive international coverage.

Each volume in the Perspectives on Modern World History series also includes:

- A full-color **world map**, offering context and geographic perspective.
- An annotated **table of contents** that provides a brief summary of each essay in the volume.
- An **introduction** specific to the volume topic.
- For each viewpoint, a brief **introduction** that has notes about the author and source of the viewpoint, and that provides a summary of its main points.
- Full-color **charts**, **graphs**, **maps**, and other visual representations.

- Informational **sidebars** that explore the lives of key individuals, give background on historical events, or explain scientific or technical concepts.
- A **glossary** that defines key terms, as needed.
- A **chronology** of important dates preceding, during, and immediately following the event.
- A **bibliography** of additional books, periodicals, and websites for further research.
- A comprehensive **subject index** that offers access to people, places, and events cited in the text.

Perspectives on Modern World History is designed for a broad spectrum of readers who want to learn more about not only history but also current events, political science, government, international relations, and sociology—students doing research for class assignments or debates, teachers and faculty seeking to supplement course materials, and others wanting to improve their understanding of history. Each volume of Perspectives on Modern World History is designed to illuminate a complicated event, to spark debate, and to show the human perspective behind the world's most significant happenings of recent decades.

INTRODUCTION

The Detroit riots were the most well-known and deadliest of 1967. Detroit was not the only city that experienced violence during that summer, however. Cincinnati; Cleveland; Washington, DC; and more than 120 other cities were also sites of riots and violence. Outside of Detroit, the largest conflict occurred in Newark, New Jersey.

The long-term causes of the Newark and Detroit riots were similar. As in Detroit, blacks in Newark were largely excluded from political offices and power. Newark mayor Hugh Addonizio had promised to appoint blacks to his administration, but failed to follow through, which stoked resentment. In one especially controversial case, the mayor chose a less-qualified white man to the school board rather than seat a black nominee. The decision almost sparked a fight between whites and blacks at a June school board meeting.

Another source of tension, again as in Detroit, was urban renewal. Urban renewal was supposed to clear slums and rundown housing to make way for highways and public buildings. In practice, it often resulted in the destruction of black neighborhoods. In early 1967, Newark city officials revealed a controversial urban renewal plan to build a hospital in the center of a black neighborhood. The hospital would take up 150 acres and force many black families from their homes. The African American community began to hold rallies against the hospital. According to a Rutgers University Web project dedicated to the riots, "Some of the same people who attended these rallies were present . . . when the riot started that summer."

The most immediate cause of the riots, however, was conflict with police. Newark's police department had a far lower percentage of whites than the city itself, and relations between the black community and police were strained. On Thursday, July 12, 1967, a cab driver named John Smith allegedly drove illegally around a double-parked police car. Smith was arrested and taken to the fourth precinct, where he was badly beaten. The precinct was near a housing project, and as news of the arrest and beating emerged, around two hundred people gathered to protest. Civil rights leaders tried to calm the crowd, but instead the protestors spread out into the city, throwing rocks and bottles and looting. Edward Williams, a black police officer, described the result:

> I saw people whom I had known for years to be law-abiding citizens caught up in the fever of lawlessness. . . . Openly, I saw a mother carrying a lamp she had taken from a store window and her young son following behind her with the matching shade. Fathers and sons were operating in teams, ripping away protective screens from liquor store windows and carting away merchandise by the cases.

As the violence moved out of black neighborhoods and into the Newark business district, the mayor called in first the New Jersey State Police, and then the National Guard. Despite the new influx of troops, or perhaps because of it, the violence increased. Black business owners—and some white ones as well—began to put up signs saying "Soul Brother" on their stores, in the (often futile) hope that looters would pass them by.

Authorities and police were initially reluctant to fire on civilians. However, as the riot dragged on—and especially after a police officer was killed by sniper fire—the reluctance to shoot diminished. On Friday, July 13, New Jersey governor Richard Hughes declared, "The line between the jungle and the law might as well be drawn here as well as any place in America," according to Newark historian Brad R. Tuttle. Tuttle adds that around a hundred civilians suffered gunshot wounds that Friday night.

The riot continued throughout the weekend. A fireman, Michael Moran, was shot from a ladder while investigating a distress call. His death resulted in further escalation by the authorities. The violence became so bad that at one point Hughes considered calling in federal troops. *New York Times* journalist Homer Bigart reported on one Saturday firefight in Newark:

> Snipers resumed fire from the upper floors of the William B. Hayes housing project in the Central Ward, using a nearby fire station as a target. A lull in the shooting had lasted until early afternoon when the looter was killed instantly by a shotgun blast. The police said he had taken a case of beer from a liquor store and was running across the street with it. One of the shotgun pellets ricocheted, hitting a 10-year-old boy, who was taken to City Hospital with an arm wound; and a National Guardsman was reported injured.

One of the more notorious deaths occurred at around midnight Sunday night, when Michael Pugh, a twelve-year-old boy, was emptying a garbage can. A friend of Michael's insulted National Guardsmen standing nearby. They opened fire, killing Michael.

Despite the New Jersey governor's suggestion that he might resort to federal troops, none were called in, and on Monday state troopers and National Guardsmen began to leave the city. Though sporadic violence continued, the riot finally quieted down. By the conclusion of the violence, twenty-three people had been killed, 235 were injured, more than 1,500 were arrested, and the city had suffered $10 million in property damage.

The Newark riots, like those in Detroit, left a mixed legacy. One unexpected result was the subsequent prominence of poet, playwright, and activist Amiri Baraka (LeRoi Jones). Baraka was a native of Newark, and was arrested, allegedly for having carried an illegal weapon and for resisting arrest. Baraka claimed to have been beaten by police while in custody, and a photograph of him handcuffed to his wheelchair with his head bandaged became a famous image of the black power movement. The photo "would be made into posters that decorated radical students' dorm room walls for decades," according to Tuttle.

Many have argued that the Newark riots damaged the city irreparably. For instance, Ann Marie Penn, whose brother was killed in the riot, said that the violence "crippled the city," as quoted in a November 19, 2006, article in *USA Today*. Others agree, arguing that the riot contributed to the exodus of white people and to economic decline. Clement Price, director of the Rutgers Institute on Ethnicity, Culture, and the Modern Experience, argues that the riots in Newark and other cities, "pretty much ended the civil rights movement."

Other commenters suggest that there was an upside to the riots' legacy. Lawrence Hamm, for example, is chair of the People's Organization for Progress, which holds a yearly commemoration of the Newark riots. Speaking to *USA Today*, he argues that "the rebellion gave rise to the political movement, gave rise to the first black mayor in Newark, the first majority black City Council." He concludes that it "pushed forward people's social consciousness." On another positive note, Gus Heningburg, a Newark civic leader, argues in a July 11, 2007, article for NJ.com "that Newark has done more to rebuild itself than any other city."

The memory of the riots continues to damage Newark's reputation, and the city still struggles with ongoing violence and high murder rates. As in Detroit, the wounds of the Newark riots have been a long time healing. *Perspectives on Modern World History: The 1967 Detroit Riots* examines the causes of the riots, the events surrounding that violent period, and the lasting impact of the uprising on the city of Detroit.

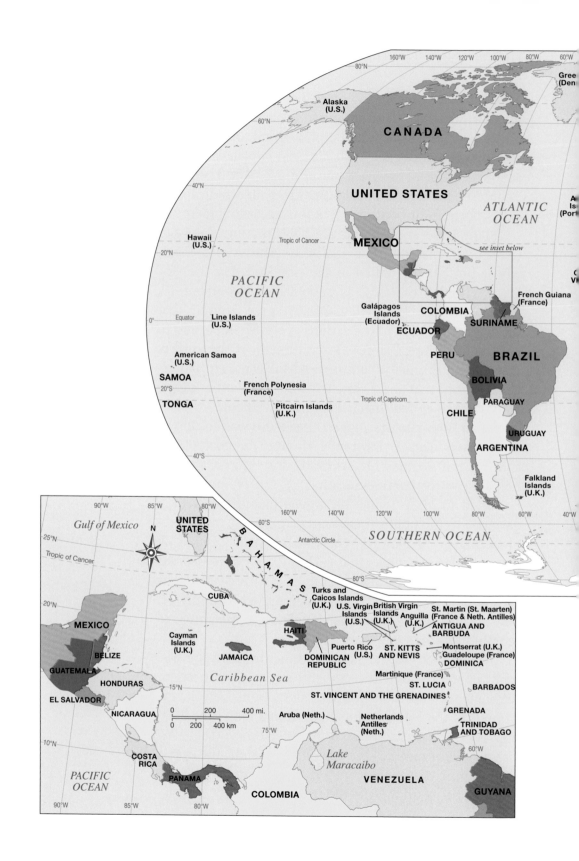

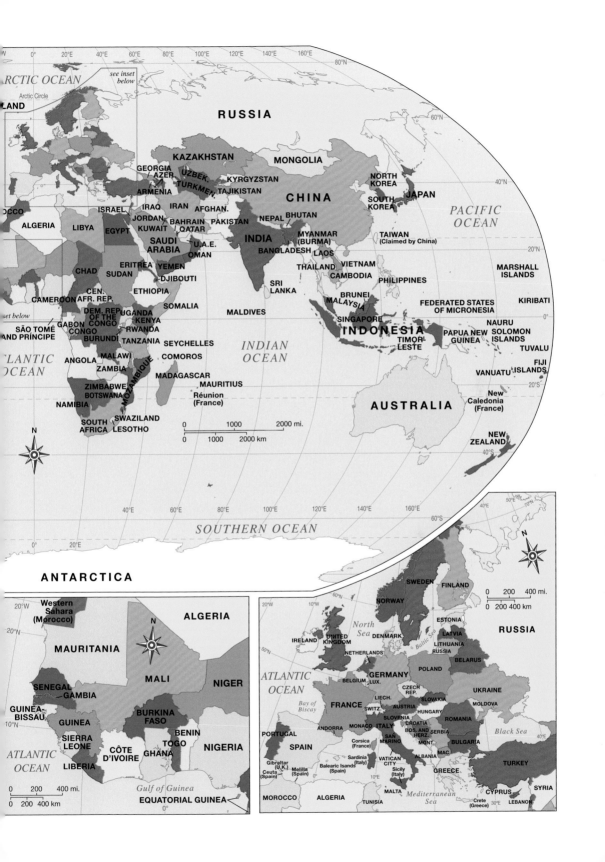

CHAPTER 1

Historical Background on the 1967 Detroit Riots

Overview of the 1967 Detroit Riots

Walter C. Rucker

In the following viewpoint, a history professor describes the events of the 1967 Detroit riots. He says the riots began with a raid on an illegal drinking club, at which many African Americans were celebrating the return of soldiers from Vietnam. The police were accused of brutality in making the arrests, which, the author maintains, sparked rioting and looting. The rioting spread and troops, including National Guardsmen and paratroopers, were called in. The author explains that most of those who died in the riots were black, and many were killed by authorities. He also links increased white flight to the riots and argues that the riots highlighted growing racial disparities in the United States. Walter C. Rucker is a professor of African and Afro-American studies at the University of North Carolina.

Photo on previous page: A middle-class African American neighborhood in Detroit lays in ruins following the 1967 riots. (© Declan Haun/ Time & Life Pictures/ Getty Images.)

SOURCE. Walter C. Rucker, "Detroit, Michigan, Riot of 1967," *Encyclopedia of African-American History*, Leslie M. Alexander and Walter C. Rucker, eds., vol. 3. Santa Barbara, CA: ABC-CLIO, 2010, pp. 741–742. Copyright © 2010 by ABC-CLIO. All rights reserved. Reproduced by permission.

In what became the deadliest urban disturbance during the 1960s, the Detroit riot of July 23–27, 1967, resulted in 43 deaths, 1,200 injuries, more than 7,000 arrests, and in excess of $300 million in damaged property. Ongoing violence, looting, arson, and gun battles convulsed the city and, for the first time in a quarter-century, the U.S. Army had to be used to contain civil strife.

The Cause of the Violence

The precipitating event leading to the violence occurred before 4 A.M. on July 23 when Detroit police raided an after-hours and illegal drinking club, referred to locally as a "blind pig," on 12th Street. A blind pig operated in open violation of city ordinances, which prohibited the sale of alcohol at bars after midnight. When the police arrived, they expected to encounter a small crowd. To their surprise, this particular blind pig had close to 80 people who were attending the celebration of two returning African American soldiers from the Vietnam War. Typically in raids on blind pigs, Detroit police would have simply arrested the proprietors and a handful of customers caught with illicit drugs. In this instance, they arrested all 73 African American patrons and the bartender. Rumors quickly spread that some of those arrested had been beaten by police officers. Given the number of individuals arrested, it took about a half-hour before police vans arrived and, in the interim, a small crowd of local residents began to gather outside the blind pig.

> Rumors of police brutality, coupled with the political volatility of the times and the depressed local economy, explains, in part, [the start of the riot].

Rumors of police brutality, coupled with the political volatility of the times and the depressed local economy, explains, in part, the events that followed. As the police vans departed with the arrested partygoers, the crowd that

formed outside the bar began throwing rocks and bricks into store windows, and about 50 people began looting a clothing store. With no police in sight, the looting spread to other nearby stores and, within an hour, dozens of stores in a 16-block radius were looted and set on fire. Within the next 24 hours, African Americans and whites in the thousands were roaming the streets, moving from Detroit's West Side to the East Side neighborhoods and into downtown. The rioters moved quickly along large sections of Grand River and Woodward Avenues and 12th Street in the downtown area of Detroit and ranged as far as seven miles toward the outer edge of the city.

Huge clouds of black smoke rise from a building in Detroit that was set on fire during the 1967 riots. (© **Rolls Press/Popperfoto/Getty Images.**)

Troops Enter the City

In an attempt to prevent the riot from spreading further, Governor [of Michigan George] Romney and Detroit

The Riots Begin

Someone in the crowd shouts, "Let's get the bricks going" as a bottle lands at the foot of an officer. Ten squad cars are on hand as the crowd jeers and mills about. More beer bottles, cans and rocks are thrown. One officer says it's getting "hairy," as police move on two rioters protected by the crowd. At 4:40 A.M., the police finish loading. Twenty minutes later, the last cruiser rolls away as an empty beer bottle arcs through the air and crashes into the rear window. The cruiser keeps going. Police are ordered out of the area. They hope the crowd will leave too.

People on the street view the retreat as a victory. A litter basket is thrown through a store window. A black youth yells, "We're going to have a riot." The crowd flows like a river down Twelfth Street. There's broken glass as the first stores are looted. Rioters steal TVs, jewelry, guns, groceries and booze from pawnshops and convenience stores. It starts with druggies, pimps and hookers, "the Cadillac and silk suit crowd," but then teenagers and 20-year-olds join in and, finally older adults. Some looters suffer cuts to their hands and legs while more experienced thieves wear gloves and hard-soled shoes. . . .

By 6:00 A.M., about 30 windows have been broken and the first looters arrested. Three squad cars—with four officers each—patrol Twelfth Street, but the police are outnumbered. When the Esquire Clothing Store is ransacked, a police car goes by with siren blaring. At least 50 looters cut and run. There are too many, so police keep going. Nearby, the owner of a shoe store watches helplessly as looters strip boxes from his shelves. Smoke billows from broken windows. Firemen arrive. People watch, some still in their nightclothes.

SOURCE: *Herb Collins,* Turning Points: The Detroit Riot of 1967: A Canadian Perspective. *Toronto, ON: Natural Heritage, 2003.*

Mayor Jerome Cavanagh acted quickly to call up 600 Detroit police, 800 state troopers, and 1,200 National Guardsmen to seal off large areas of the city and to disperse the rioters. These actions were not sufficient and the violence of the riot intensified. By Monday, July 24, the first three fatalities of the riot occurred. All three were white. One was beaten to death by a group of African American youths while protecting his store. Another was killed by a stray bullet. The third was a rioter killed by a storeowner. Ironically, the vast majority of those killed during the five full days of rioting were African American, and many of their deaths are attributed to the police and National Guard.

> "The vast majority of those killed during the five full days of rioting were African American, and many of their deaths are attributed to the police and National Guard."

When it became clear that local and state law enforcement resources were insufficient, Governor Romney requested federal assistance from U.S. Attorney General Ramsey Clark. Clark informed Romney that before federal troops could be sent, the governor had to declare that a civil insurrection was taking place. Romney balked at this, fearing that insurance companies would not compensate residents of Detroit for their property losses if the cause was insurrection. When the situation in the city became progressively worse, President Lyndon Baines Johnson stepped in and sent Army paratroopers from the 101st Airborne.

While the paratroopers assisted in restoring order to the city, a number of disturbing incidents occurred that further enraged African American residents in Detroit. In one incident, National Guardsmen fired .50-caliber machine gun rounds into an apartment building, killing a four-year-old girl. In a more publicized case, three unarmed African American teenagers—Aubrey Pollard, Fred Temple, and Carl Cooper—were shot and killed at

Algiers Motel by three Detroit police officers. The three officers were later exonerated by an all-white jury, and two of them returned to the police force by 1971.

By Thursday, July 27, the riot was effectively over and federal paratroopers were withdrawn. President Johnson appointed a Special Advisor Commission on Civil Disorders on July 27, 1967 to help discern the origins of the Detroit riot and other civil disturbances occurring during the so-called long, hot summer of 1967. Pointing to economic disparities and despair in urban "ghettoes," the commission headed by Illinois Governor Otto Kerner concluded that America was sharply divided into two societies—one white, one black—which were separate and increasingly unequal. In the aftermath of the riot, white flight to the suburbs of Detroit accelerated at an alarming rate to the point that the city had a majority African American population by the early 1970s. The removal of whites to Detroit's suburbs and the creation of an impoverished and black urban core provided additional proof of the Kerner Commission's assessments of the growing economic and even spatial divides in the United States.

President Johnson Explains Why He Is Sending Troops into Detroit

Lyndon Baines Johnson

In the following viewpoint, the president of the United States explains that he has ordered federal troops into Detroit, because local and state authorities have been unable to handle the rioting. He says that the rioting and lawlessness have nothing to do with the civil rights struggle, and he notes that the vast majority of people, black and white, deplore the violence and rioting. He concludes by asking citizens to help the government maintain order by staying off the streets and supporting the efforts of law enforcement. Lyndon B. Johnson was president of the United States from 1963 to 1969.

SOURCE. Lyndon Baines Johnson, "Address After Ordering Federal Troops to Detroit, Michigan," Miller Center, July 24, 1967.

At 10:56 this morning [July 24, 1967], I received a wire from Governor [of Michigan George] Romney officially requesting that Federal troops be dispatched to Michigan. This wire had been sent at 10:46 A.M.

At 11:02 A.M. this morning, I instructed the Secretary of Defense, Mr. [Robert] McNamara, to initiate the movement of the troops which the Governor had requested.

At the same time, I advised the Governor by telegram that the troops would be sent to Selfridge Air Base just northeast of Detroit and would be available to support and to assist the some 8,000 Michigan National Guardsmen and the several thousand State and local police under the command of Governor Romney and the mayor of Detroit. I informed the Governor that these troops would arrive this afternoon.

President Lyndon Johnson (seated) meets with senior staff in the Oval Office of the White House as he prepares to order federal troops to Detroit to quell the race riots. (© **Corbis**.)

I also informed the Governor that immediately Mr. Cyrus Vance, as Special Assistant to the Secretary of Defense, and others would proceed to Detroit for conferences with the Governor and other appropriate officials.

This plan proceeded precisely as scheduled. Approximately 5,000 Federal troops were on their way by airlift to Detroit, Michigan, within a few hours. Mr. Vance, General [John L.] Throckmorton, and others were in Detroit and in conference with Governor Romney by the middle of this afternoon.

Assessing the Situation

Their initial report was that it then appeared that the situation might be controlled without bringing the Federal troops from the Selfridge Air Force Base into downtown Detroit. They, therefore, recommended to the President that the troops be maintained on a 30-minute alert and they advised that they would be in continual touch with the situation and with Secretary McNamara and me, making periodic reports about every 30 minutes.

At approximately 10:30 this evening, Mr. Vance and General Throckmorton reported to me by telephone that it was the unanimous opinion of all the State and Federal officials who were in consultation—including Governor Romney, Mr. Vance, General Throckmorton, the mayor, and others—that the situation had developed in such a way in the few intervening hours as to make the use of Federal troops to augment the police and Michigan National Guard imperative. They described the situation in considerable detail, including the violence and deaths that had occurred in the past few hours, and submitted as the unanimous judgment of all concerned that the situation was totally beyond the control of the local authorities.

> The situation was totally beyond the control of the local authorities.

On the basis of this confirmation of the need for participation by Federal troops, and pursuant to the official request made by the Governor of the State of Michigan, in which Mayor [Jerome] Cavanagh of Detroit joined, I forthwith issued the necessary proclamation and Executive order as provided by the Constitution and the statutes.

Deploying Troops Is the Last Resort

I advised Mr. Vance and General Throckmorton to proceed immediately with the transportation of the Federal troops from Selfridge Air Force Base to places of deployment within Detroit—a movement which they had already provisionally begun, pursuant to their authority.

I am sure the American people will realize that I take this action with the greatest regret—and only because of the clear, unmistakable, and undisputed evidence that Governor Romney of Michigan and the local officials in Detroit have been unable to bring the situation under control.

> "Pillage, looting, murder, and arson have nothing to do with civil rights. They are criminal conduct."

Law enforcement is a local matter. It is the responsibility of local officials and the Governors of the respective States. The Federal Government should not intervene—except in the most extraordinary circumstances.

The fact of the matter, however, is that law and order have broken down in Detroit, Michigan.

Pillage, looting, murder, and arson have nothing to do with civil rights. They are criminal conduct. The Federal Government in the circumstances here presented had no alternative but to respond, since it was called upon by the Governor of the State and since it was presented with proof of his inability to restore order in Michigan.

We will not tolerate lawlessness. We will not endure violence. It matters not by whom it is done or under what slogan or banner. It will not be tolerated. This Nation will do whatever it is necessary to do to suppress and to punish those who engage in it.

I know that with few exceptions the people of Detroit, and the people of Newark, and the people of Harlem, and of all of our American cities, however troubled they may be, deplore and condemn these criminal acts. I know that the vast majority of Negroes and whites are shocked and outraged by them.

So tonight, your President calls upon all of our people, in all of our cities, to join in a determined program to maintain law and order—to condemn and to combat lawlessness in all of its forms—and firmly to show by word and by deed that riots, looting, and public disorder will just not be tolerated.

In particular, I call upon the people of the ravaged areas to return to their homes, to leave the streets, and to permit the authorities to restore quiet and order without further loss of life or property damage. Once this is done, attention can immediately be turned to the great and urgent problems of repairing the damage that has been done.

I appeal to every American in this grave hour to respond to this plea.

Congress Struggles to Respond to Urban Rioting

Chalmers M. Roberts

In the following viewpoint, a journalist discusses the national political reactions and implications of the Detroit riots. The author reports that both Republicans and Democrats tried to blame each other for the riots. He says that there was especially tension between the Democratic president Lyndon Johnson and the Republican Michigan governor George Romney, who was discussing plans to run against Johnson for president. He also reports on rumors that the riot was incited by Communists and on heated rhetoric from some in Congress who advocated shooting rioters. Chalmers M. Roberts was a longtime correspondent for the *Washington Post*.

Republican leaders yesterday [July 25, 1967] pressed for a major congressional investigation of urban rioting as members of both parties traded political charges in a verbal eruption on Capitol Hill and elsewhere in the Nation.

Talk of Conspiracy

There was talk of conspiracy, Communist or otherwise, behind the rioting. From all sides came expressions of anger and frustration over the breakdown of law and order in Detroit, Cambridge, Md., and elsewhere in the midst of a long summer of Negro discontent.

> 'Tremendous problems of fear and resentment are being created with the white community.'

The charges and blame-placing were an obvious prelude to next year's [1968] presidential campaign, though it was too early to judge who has been hurt most by the rioting. Probably few would quarrel with Sen. Jacob K. Javits (R-N.Y.), who said that "tremendous problems of fear and resentment are being created with the white community."

Senate GOP Leader Everett M. Dirksen (Ill.) and House Leader Gerald R. Ford (Mich.) introduced bills to set up a joint investigation of the rioting, its causes, whether there has been a conspiracy to incite and provoke civil disorders and whether the riots have been organized or encouraged by Communists or other subversive groups.

Senate Democratic Leader Mike Mansfield (Mont.), while approving a joint inquiry, indicated he would prefer that President Johnson set up a panel. The White House said that was the Senator's idea, not the President's.

But House Democratic Leader Carl Albert (Okla.) said of the Republican move that "after their statement yesterday (blaming the President for the riots) I'm inclined to be suspicious of anything they say or do on this

The Political Career of George Romney

As president and chairman of the American Motors Corporation in the 1950s, George Romney (1907–1995) transformed the US auto industry by putting the first compact car on the market. Later, after serving as a three-term governor of Michigan, he was thrust into the national arena and considered seeking the presidential nomination in 1968.

The career of George Romney is long and diverse. He worked as a sugar harvester as a child, was a Mormon missionary in his 20s, led a struggling automobile company, governed an industrial state for three terms, and served in President Richard Nixon's cabinet. He wore many hats and, as was said by his colleague John H. Chafee, former governor of Rhode Island, "in each of these he has been a success." . . .

In 1968 Romney considered the 1968 presidential nomination, but called being the governor of Michigan "a priceless experience." His friend, and fellow state governor John H. Chafee, stated, "The Republican Party, but even more the nation, has reason to be grateful that a man of George Romney's ability, energy, and integrity is willing to come forward to serve the people. His is the

subject." Albert suggested that the FBI ought to do the investigating.

Dirksen told newsmen that although he and Mr. Johnson had ridden together to and from the funeral yesterday of Navy Secretary-designate John T. McNaughton, they did not discuss the proposed investigation. Saying he did not want the probe to "become a political football," Dirksen declared that he thought the Senate Judiciary Committee today would consider the House-passed antiriot bill.

Democrats Introduce a Bill

Two Democratic Senators, Fred R. Harris (Okla.) and Walter F. Mondale (Minn.), introduced a bill to establish a blue-ribbon committee of nine, to be composed of members from the executive, legislative and executive leadership we need on a national level." Others considered him an outside shot at best. But while on the television program, "Meet the Press," on October 15, 1967, Romney countered with, "I'm used to being an underdog. I've been an underdog in everything I've gone into of consequence throughout my life."

In the end, two events kept Romney from making a serious run for the White House. [Historian George S.] May wrote that Romney "probably forfeited whatever chances he may have had of gaining the Republican presidential nomination in 1968 when he alienated many in his party by coming out against the [Vietnam] War." May continued that "earlier, in the summer of 1967, Romney's political hopes had been damaged by riots in Detroit." Property damage reached at least $50 million. Governor Romney, Detroit's mayor [Jerome Cavanagh], and President [Lyndon] Johnson were all criticized for their reactions to this tragedy, which had an adverse effect on their political careers.

SOURCE: *"George Romney,"* Encyclopedia of World Biography, *vol. 20. Detroit, MI: Gale, 2000.*

branches, as was the Warren Commission on the [John F.] Kennedy assassination.

Thus it was uncertain last night just what would emerge in the way of an investigation. But that did not halt the political thrust and counterthrust.

Politics was evident at two levels: in the exchanges between President Johnson and Gov. George Romney of Michigan, who may be his opponent in 1968, and in the crossfire of congressional comment that followed the Republican Coordinating Committee's statement of Monday putting much of the blame on the President.

Mr. Johnson's midnight television statement repeatedly put the responsibility on Romney for the use of Federal troops. The President said he had acted "only because of the clear, unmistakable and undisputed evidence that Gov. Romney and the local officials have been unable to bring the situation under control."

Michigan governor George Romney (center) and Detroit mayor Jerome Cavanagh (right) confer during the riots, as a National Guardsman stands by. (© AP Images.)

Romney obviously felt this was a political thrust. . . .

There also was controversy as to whether the President had acted quickly enough. Romney apparently felt not. When asked about the delay, he replied:

"You'll have to ask them, but I think it's the usual thing."

Washington Post staff writer Andrew J. Glass, in reporting this from Detroit, said Romney meant to imply the delay was due to political reasons.

White House press secretary George E. Christian conceded that "There was a public difference of views" on Monday evening on the need for the troops. They were not sent until the President's emissary on the spot, former Deputy Defense Secretary Cyrus Vance, advised in favor. That was after both Romney and Mayor Jerome Cavanagh had said they were needed.

"Playing Presidential Politics"

Rep. Charles C. Diggs Jr. (D-Mich.) said yesterday that he had intervened with a phone call to the President, urging that troops be sent into the city. Diggs said he was "quite aware of the political implications involved" in the use of Federal troops.

However, Christian later said the orders permitting the use of the troops had already been issued by the time Diggs said he called. Diggs took the position that the rioting constituted "a civil insurrection."

The GOP statement aimed at the President brought some hot retorts yesterday. Albert asked on the floor: "Why was Romney so slow in making his request? Was it because he was afraid of losing support in his attempt to become the next President?"

Democratic Whip Hale Boggs (La.) said it was "the height of irresponsibility" to blame the President, and Rep. Wayne L. Hays (D-Ohio) called the statement "the most blatant piece of political propaganda that I have seen in my life." Hays accused Romney of "playing presidential politics."

The National League of Cities put out a statement defending Mr. Johnson and saying that "the very Republicans who now condemn the President and decry the current unrest have consistently opposed these constructive programs and slashed their appropriations." Mansfield said much the same thing.

Ford, who along with Dirksen was a member of the group that approved the GOP statement, commented that the Democrats had been the first to introduce politics by slapping the Republicans after the Newark (N.J.) riots for not supporting Administration bills. He added that it is "our prerogative to hit back."

Shifting the Blame

Ford also confirmed reports that the GOP statement's reference to factories manufacturing Molotov cocktails for rioters was based on information from former Gov. Thomas E. Dewey of New York, twice the GOP presidential candidate, who got it from a newspaper story.

Sen. Robert F. Kennedy (D.-N.Y.) spoke yesterday of "the gravest crisis" in domestic affairs since the Civil War, adding that "wherever violence and mob action breaks out, it must be stopped forthwith."

> Adult looters, said [Senator Robert C.] Byrd, 'should be shot on the spot.'

The toughest language came from Sen. Robert C. Byrd (D-W.Va.), who said "insurrection" in the cities "should be put down with brute force." Adult looters, said Byrd, "should be shot on the spot." Criticizing some Negroes for avoiding work, Byrd added:

"All you have to do is travel six blocks from the Capitol building and look at the young hoodlums on street corners, listen to their language, and you understand the reluctance of employers to give them jobs."

Byrd's remarks were commended by Sen. Harry F. Byrd Jr. (D-Va.) and Sen. Russell B. Long (D.-La.)

During 90 minutes of House speeches on the rioting, Rep. Louis C. Wyman (R-N.H.) introduced legislation to take away all Federal benefits from anyone who riots.

Rep. Joe D. Waggonner Jr. (D-La.) blamed Congress for passing civil rights legislation and Rep. Jamie L. Whitten (D-Miss.) put the blame on the Supreme Court.

By coincidence, former President [Dwight D.] Eisenhower, in a *Reader's Digest* article released yesterday, said recent Court decisions have "gravely handicapped" the police and have "helped tilt the scales against effective law enforcement." He endorsed the idea of a constitutional amendment "to restore the powers of the police" if it is necessary.

The former President said that while he had "the utmost sympathy for any person who has never had a decent chance in life, the fact that society has treated him badly does not give him the right to smash a store window and take what he wants, or to attack our police with animal ferocity."

Police Terrorize Citizens in the Algiers Motel

John Hersey

In the following viewpoint, a journalist reports on the Algiers Motel incident, in which three black men were murdered and numerous other people were beaten in a Detroit motel by police and members of the US National Guard following reports of gunshots fired in the motel. Based on witness interviews and forensic reports, the author reconstructs the events that took place in the Algiers Motel. John Hersey was a writer and journalist and the author of *Hiroshima*.

"Then," Lee [Forsythe, a witness] said to me, "they started killing us one by one."

SOURCE. John Hersey, "27: The Death Game," *The Algiers Motel Incident*, pp. 273–276. Originally published by Alfred A. Knopf. Copyright © 1968 by John Hersey, renewed 1996 by Brook Hersey. Reprinted by permission of Brook Hersey and the Barbara Day Hersey Trust. All rights reserved.

"They were going to shoot us," Michael [Clark, a witness] testified, "one at a time."

Scaring the Witnesses

"One of the Detroit officers," [National Guardsman warrant officer Theodore] Thomas told the police, "pulled the 'big man'"—Roderick Davis—"out of the line and took him in A-4." In court Thomas was more explicit, "Officer [David] Senak," he testified, "took the first man out of the line . . . into the front room, one to the left in front." "When they went in," [Robert] Greene told [prosecutor Jesse] Eggleton, "he closed the door." Roderick Davis said to me, "They told me, 'Lie on the floor face down, and if you make a move or say a word we'll kill you.'" "I followed them to the doorway," Warrant Officer Thomas testified, "and Officer Senak told the man to lay on the floor and he fired a round through the wall. I seen him point the gun to the other direction. He didn't shoot him. He scared him. . . . He winked at me. He didn't say nothing." "I thought," Roderick testified, "he shot in the floor because I felt like vibration reaction by my feet." "In the floor or through a chair or something," Roderick said to me.

Attorney [Konrad] Kohl: "Now, you were in a room with David Senak when he took a prisoner in there?"

Warrant Officer Thomas: "Yes, sir."

Kohl: "And is it not true that he told the man to lie down on the floor? He fired a shot but he didn't shoot at the man, did he?"

Thomas: "Definitely not."

Senak fired, Thomas testified, "right in the corner."

"He looked at me," Thomas testified, "and winked, indicating it was all right. . . . When we took the first man in I realized what he was doing. And it was better than letting these people be beaten; seriously. I felt somebody was going to really get hurt seriously, and I felt this was the best thing at the time."

> 'They said, "Don't budge an inch or you'll be dead."'

"Then," Roderick told me, "they said, 'Don't budge an inch or you'll be dead.'" And the men left him alone in the room.

Want to Kill One?

"The warrant officer," Greene told Eggleton, "came out, and the policeman asked the other officer, 'Did he kill him?' And the officer said, 'Yes.'" This was for the ears of the people in the line.

"This officer . . ." the Thomas synopsis said, "asked Thomas if he wanted to kill one. Thomas said, 'Yes,' and took one of the men"—Michael Clark—"into A-4 and fired a rifle shot into the ceiling, forcing the man to remain in the room."

"I also took one person into that front room," Thomas testified. ". . . I used my M-1 rifle. . . . I also told the man to lay on the floor, and fired a round through the ceiling . . . toward the corner so that anybody upstairs wouldn't get hit. I didn't think there was anybody upstairs around at the corner of the house."

"Let's see," Michael testified, "[Policeman Ronald] August"—once again he seems to err; even Senak's lawyer placed Senak in this role—"told the soldier to shoot me or something. Anyway, the soldier told me to lay down. Then he shot. I think he shot out the window or in the hall somewhere. Then he told me just to lay there and be quiet. And he said if I make any noise, he [is] going to come back and shoot me for real."

Announcing an Intent to Kill

"Clark and an unknown man were taken into room A-4," the [witness James] Sortor synopsis says of this first phase of the death game, "shots were heard, and the officers returned, saying, 'We killed those two.'" Telling me the story, Sortor said, "And so they said they were going to kill us, you know. They said they were going to kill us n-----s, you know, so they picked Michael and this other guy out, so they said they were going to kill these two n-----s, so they took them in this room in there, we heard two shots, so the police come out, so he said, 'I killed them two motherf---ers.'"

> 'They said they were going to kill these two n----s, so they took them in this room in there, we heard two shots.'

[Witness] Karen [Malloy] told the detectives "she believed the police killed Michael Clark." From the synopsis of [witness] Juli Hysell's statement: "They . . . made Hysell believe Clark was dead."

Rational, Reasonable Explanation

Thomas testified, "Immediately after the officer shot into the wall, into the floor, or corner, or wherever you want to call it, and laid the man down, they"—the people against the wall—"thought this man had been shot and they were willing to talk. . . . I believe it was one of the girls—I wouldn't swear to it—said, 'Why don't you tell him about the gun? Carl [Cooper] is dead anyway.' And this is one of the statements I specifically heard to this effect."

"One boy spoke up," Juli testified, "and said that the boy that was dead was the one that had the pistol, and that's the only thing that was said to my knowledge about the pistol."

"One of the persons" Karen told [attorney] Allen Early, "who had been in A-2 & come up to A-4 said, 'Go on and tell them anything because they've already killed him.' This was with reference to the blank pistol. This other person then said, 'The guy in there on the floor' (referring to Carl in A-2) 'had a blank pistol.' Policeman

The bodies of three shooting victims are removed from the Algiers Motel on July 27, 1967. (© AP Images.)

said, 'Why didn't you tell us that before we killed the other guy?'"

Having elicited from Juli, in the conspiracy hearing, an estimate that the ordeal in the hallway had been going on for about twenty minutes before this first mention of the starter pistol, Attorney Kohl asked her, "Now, if in fact there was simply a blank pistol that had been fired, will you advise this Court, please, what rational, reasonable explanation there could be for not telling the police who would have the gun and who had done what for a period of twenty minutes?"

Juli answered: "Because everybody was scared."

Who's Killed Next?

Karen told Early, "The talking policeman then said, 'Who shall we get next?'"

The Victims of the Detroit Riots

The Detroit and Newark Riots of 1967

The following viewpoint lists the people killed during the Detroit riots and the circumstances of their deaths. The viewpoint describes many incidents in which people were shot for looting, in some cases possibly by mistake. People were also shot, according to the viewpoint, when it was thought they were engaging in sniper fire; in one such incident, a four-year-old was accidentally shot when a relative lit a match for a cigarette in a darkened building. One police officer was killed during the riot. In the case of many of the deaths, the viewpoint maintains, no one was prosecuted or convicted. *The Detroit and Newark Riots of 1967* is a website organized by Max Herman, an assistant professor of sociology at New Jersey City University.

Krikor "George" Messerlian died 7/27/67 as a result of injuries sustained on 7/23/67 around 2:30 P.M. A 68-year-old Armenian immigrant, Messerlian died while defending his shoe repair shop located at

SOURCE. Max Herman, Assistant Professor of Sociology, New Jersey City University. Reproduced by permission.

7711 Linwood Ave near 12th Street. He was beaten by a group of black youths, one wielding a baseball bat. Messerlian had attempted to fight them off with an old ceremonial saber. Police charged a 20-year-old boy who had recently moved from Alabama with Messerlian's death.

Willie Hunter and Prince Williams of 1734 Seward died 7/23/67 sometime during the evening. Hunter, age 26, and Williams, age 32, both African American, originally from Alabama and Georgia respectively, worked together at a Detroit auto plant. On July 23rd, both men were observed walking in the vicinity of Brown's Drug Store, located at 8202 12th Street. On July 26th, their badly burned bodies were found in the basement of that store, which had been destroyed by fire. Police reports indicated that they were asphyxiated by carbon monoxide as a result of the fire. It is suspected that they were looting the store at the time the fire broke out.

Sheren George died 7/24/67 at 1:45 A.M. A 23-year-old, white mother of two who worked as an exotic dancer, Sheren was shot while riding in the front seat of a car driven by her husband, Ross. As the car headed north on Woodward Avenue near Melbourne, around 11:30 P.M., Mrs. George, her husband, and a friend, Paul Dimitrie, observed a white man being beaten by a crowd of black youths. As they slowed down, and attempted to exit the area, a shot was fired, which hit Mrs. George in the left side below her breast and glanced off her husband. She died at Detroit General Hospital a few hours later.

Julius Dorsey died 7/25/67 at 1:30 A.M. Dorsey, a 55-year-old black male, originally from Memphis, Tennessee, worked as a security guard at a small grocery store at the corner of Field and Lafayette. He was reportedly shot by National Guardsmen who were in the process of pursuing suspected looters at the time.

Clifton Pryor died 7/24/67 at 4:00 A.M. Pryor, a 23-year-old white male migrant worker from Tennessee who did roofing work, was killed while carrying a mop and bucket on the roof of his apartment at 667 Alexandrine. He and some other residents had gone to the roof to protect the building from sparks associated with nearby fires. Mistaken for a sniper, Pryor was shot by a National Guardsman. The official police report still lists Pryor as a "sniper."

John Ashby died 8/4/67 of injuries sustained on 7/24/67 at 7 A.M. Ashby, a 26-year-old white male, served as a firefighter with the Detroit Fire Department, Engine 21. He was electrocuted by a high-tension wire that struck his helmet while fighting a fire at a supermarket at Lafayette and Canton on Detroit's East Side. He died a few weeks later at Detroit General Hospital as a result of burns and infection.

Herman Ector died 7/24/67 at 10:05 A.M. Ector, a 30-year-old black male, Detroit native, star athlete, and former high school class president, was shot by a security guard in front of Lindy's Supermarket, 3745 Joy Road. An army veteran and auto worker, Herman and his brother Vincent intervened in a dispute between a group of youths and a security guard, Waverly Solomon, whom Ector felt was treating the youths roughly. When Ector commented to a friend that, "he (Solomon) ought to stop treating them like that," the security guard said "Who the hell are you talking to?" and then shot Ector with his carbine rifle. Solomon was initially charged with Ector's murder, but the charges were later dropped.

Fred Williams died 7/24/67 at 8 A.M. Williams, a 49-year-old black male, originally from Arkansas, worked in construction. He was especially proud to have purchased his own home at 9541 Goodwin St. When the store on the corner near his home was set on fire, Mr. Williams feared it might spread and began to move his family's personal effects away from the house. As he moved his clothes, he stepped on a downed power line and was killed. His home subsequently burned down.

Daniel Jennings died 7/24/67 at 1:15 P.M. Jennings, a 36-year-old black man, native Detroiter and father of 14, had recently lost his job as a wrecker at a local salvage yard. On Sunday, he decided to go for a walk. His journey took him to Stanley's Patent Medicine and Package Store, which was closed. As he and three others broke into the building, he was shot by the owner, Stanley Meszezenski.

Robert Beal died 7/24/67 at 1:25 P.M. Beal, a forty-nine-year-old black man, originally from Arkansas, had lost his job as a truck driver/mechanic for Pontiac Motors. On Sunday, he drove around town to see what was happening. He was shot by a Detroit Police officer at a burned out auto parts store located at 8857 Treadwell where police and National Guardsmen were patrolling. Police claim he was inside the building and resisted orders to halt. Other witnesses state that he was shot outside the shop. The police report lists him officially as a "looter."

Joseph Chandler died 7/24/67 at 1:45 P.M. Chandler, a 34-year-old black, unemployed former auto worker, had migrated to Detroit from Kentucky. He was shot by police while engaged in looting at the Food Time Market, 8360 2nd Street. Exiting through a broken window with handfuls of groceries, Chandler was commanded by police to halt, but fled and was subsequently shot.

Herman Canty died 7/24/67 at 2:45 P.M. Canty, a 46-year-old black man and native of Georgia, worked at a local car wash. According to the police report, Canty was observed loading merchandise from the rear door of the Bi-Lo Supermarket at 2450 West Grand Blvd into a truck parked nearby. As police arrived, Canty jumped into the truck and drove off. Police fired several rounds at the truck until it stopped. Canty was slumped at the wheel with a gunshot wound to his neck. Police claim that in addition to looting the supermarket, Canty had tossed a firebomb in the building.

Alfred Peachlum, a 35-year-old African American male, died at 4 P.M. on 7/24/67 as a result of shots fired by Patrolmen Charles Carlson and James Lozon. Peachlum, a father of three and an avid baseball fan, was employed as a welder at a General Motors Plant. On this fateful day, Peachlum decided to inspect the area to see the damage that had been done. His journey took him to A&P supermarket at 3430 Joy Road where there was looting underway. Peachlum was in the store when the police arrived. Upon seeing the officers, Peachlum ran for the door. Peachlum had a shiny object in his hand. The policemen thought it was a gun. They opened fire, killing Peachlum. The object turned out to be a piece of meat wrapped in shiny paper.

Alphonso Smith, a 35-year-old African American male, died 7/24/67 around 5 P.M. of gunshot wounds received from police while allegedly looting a supermarket. Smith was well respected in his community and lived in a fashionable upscale apartment. The police version of the incident was that Smith and four other men were cornered while looting the Standard Food Market at 9750 Dexter. Upon realizing that he was cornered, Smith allegedly threw something at an officer, who started to fire wildly with his machine gun, causing another officer to slip on the floor and accidentally discharge his weapon, which killed Smith. Other sources claim that the officer fired through a window. No one was held criminally responsible for the crime. It was ruled an "Accidental shooting" on the police report.

Nathaniel Edmonds, a 23-year-old African American male, died at 4:20 P.M. on 7/24/67 from gunshots fired by Richard Shugar, a 24-year-old white male. Edmonds was sitting [in] his backyard at 7714 Harper when a car driven by Shugar passed by. Shugar accused Edmonds of breaking into his store. When Edmonds denied the allegation, an argument ensued. Shugar went to the trunk of the 1969 red Oldsmobile and grabbed a shotgun, which he then used to shoot Edmonds in his chest. Shugar was charged with first-degree murder.

Charles Kemp, a 35-year-old African American male, died 7/24/67 at 5:20 P.M. as a result of injuries received from shots fired by two policemen and a National Guard sergeant. Kemp, a father of two and former gas station attendant, was shot because he took five packs of cigars and was observed removing a cash register from Borgi's market at 1800 Mack. The lawmen arrived just as Kemp was making his escape. He ran, the police officers in the squad car gave chase, and shots were fired. A few minutes later, Kemp's body was found riddled with bullets to his back and his knees. He apparently was shot while running.

Richard Sims, a 35-year-old African American male, died 7/24/67 at 9:20 P.M. as a result of gunshot wounds. Sims, a former employee of Chrysler Motor Company, was allegedly shot after he attempted to break into the Hobby Bar at 13106 Linwood, near his house. While in the process of breaking into the bar, police officers arrived on the scene. [Sims] then ran. The police officers claim they gave instructions to stop. [Sims] refused, so they shot him. No weapon was found on his body. Nobody was held criminally responsible for his death.

John Leroy, a 30-year-old African American male who lived at 5119 Garland, died 7/24/67 around 11:30 P.M. According to the official police report, Leroy was a passenger in a vehicle that failed to stop at [a] roadblock erected by the National Guard and police. Other sources claimed that the men came upon a jeep in the middle of the road, so they stopped the car. Then the men in the jeep opened fire at the occupants of the car. They screamed out for help but to no avail. All four passengers had been shot. Leroy's fellow passengers survived the attack but Leroy did not.

Carl Smith, a 30-year-old white male firefighter, died 7/25/67 at 12:50 A.M. Carl Smith had worked for the Detroit Fire Department for five years and reportedly was a good father to his kids. He did not hesitate to join the fire team as they attempted to restore calm to the riot area. Smith was attempting [to] organize units at Mack and St. Jean to quell some of the fires. At that point, gunshots were fired and chaos broke out. At the end of the gunfire, Smith was lying dead on the ground. It is unclear who fired the shots that killed Smith. Nobody was held criminally responsible for his death.

Emanuel Cosby, a 26-year-old African American male, died 7/25/67 at 1:04 A.M. Cosby, a product of the Detroit ghetto and a soldier during the Korean War, took the opportunity to loot like many others did during the Detroit riot. On the encouragement of his friends, Cosby took a tire iron and decided to break into N&T Market at 4441 E. Nevada. Unfortunately for Cosby, the police arrived just as he was making his escape. Upon sighting the policeman, Cosby began to run. He was shot while running away with the loot in his possession.

Henry Denson, a 27-year-old African American male, died 7/25/67 at 2:10 A.M. as a result of gunshots wounds fired by National Guardsmen. Denson was a passenger in a car with two other black males when they came upon roadblocks erected by National Guardsmen at Mack and East Grand Blvd. The Guardsmen shouted instructions to stop, but before the driver could comply with the orders, they opened fire. A gunshot came through the windscreen of the car and tore through Denson's neck. The men had no weapons in their possession. The official police report claims that the driver had attempted to run over the lawmen.

Jerome Olshove was, from all indications, a cop with a bright future until his life was ended on 7/25/67 at 3:35 A.M. Olshove was a member of the Detroit Police Department for eight years. He was the only policeman killed in the riot. It was around 3 A.M. on Tuesday morning when the National Guard fired shots into A&P supermarket at 121 Holbrook. Olshove then arrived at the scene with several other officers. Only a few looters remained in the store. They were instructed to surrender. One man, Charles Latimer, voluntarily surrendered, but the other man, Danny Royster, resisted. A scuffle ensued between Royster and another officer, Patrolman Roy St. Onge. As Royster attempted to grab for St. Onge's shotgun, the gun discharged, wounding Officer Olshove who was standing nearby. Royster and Latimer were charged with first-degree murder, although evidence suggests that Olshove's death was an accident.

William Jones and Ronald Evans, a 28-year-old African American male and a 24-year-old black male, died 7/25/67 at 3:45 A.M. A native of Alabama, Jones died as a result of gunshot wounds received while looting a liquor store. Jones and Evans, who had just turned 24, decided to break into a liquor store on his block at 4100 Pennsylvania. The police were alerted to the men who were stealing beer. Jones and Evans ran when the saw the police.

Orders were given to halt, but the men continued to run, so the officers opened fire. Jones and Evans were found alongside each other. Evans had been shot 14 times by the police.

Roy Banks, a 46-year-old African American male, died 7/27/67 at 4:30 A.M. Banks was a deaf mute who led a pretty simple life as a laborer at a fabricating plant and was not a troublemaker. He was walking to the bus stop at Rohns and Mack on his way to work when he was shot down by a National Guardsman. It is unclear how Banks ended up in that street. The official police report claims that Banks was a looter and was running away from the scene of a crime when he was shot. However, other sources claim that Banks was walking along the street when he was shot by Guardsmen without provocation. The Guardsmen, contrary to the police report, did not give orders to halt. They just opened fire. The place that Banks was allegedly looting was still fully intact. . . .

Frank Tanner, a 19-year-old African American male, died 7/25/67 at 8:05 A.M. Tanner was formerly employed at a Laundromat, but was unemployed at the time of his death when he [was] shot as a suspected looter. Tanner and his friends decided to break into a store at 1481 E. Grand Blvd. and proceeded to load a box with liquor. While the men were making their escape, a National Guardsman came down the street and instructed everybody to be still. When people scattered, the Guardsmen opened fire, hitting Tanner. Tanner managed to make it to a nearby alley, where he was found dead by a passerby. No one was held criminally responsible for his death.

Arthur Johnson and Perry Williams, both 36-year-old black men, died 7/25/67 at 3:25 P.M. Johnson and Williams, who were both high school dropouts, were also best friends. They eventually died together. Johnson and Williams were hanging around a pawnshop at 1401 Holbrook that had been looted and burned. Upon seeing the police coming down the street, they ran into the store. The officers sprayed the store with gunshots and kept driving. After those officers left the scene, another contingent of policemen arrived and entered the building. At this point, officers claim that Johnson and Williams attacked them with clubs. As result, they shot both Johnson and Williams, allegedly in self-defense. The policemen claimed they had received a radio call to the shop but the police log suggested otherwise.

Jack Snydor, a 38-year-old African American male, died 7/25/67 at 9:15 P.M. In a state of intoxication, he fired a pistol out his window at 2753 Hazelwood Apt. #32. This shot was interpreted by neighbors as sniper fire. The police and National Guard were alerted. They came and surrounded the building. When Patrolman Roger Poike broke down the door to Snydor's apartment, Snydor shot the policeman. In response, police fired a barrage of bullets into in the apartment. Racked with bullets, Snydor's body fell three floors to the pavement below. Newspaper reports referred to him as a "sniper."

Tanya Blanding, a 4-year-old African American female, died 7/26/67 at 12:30 A.M. Tanya was the youngest and most innocent victim of the riot. Tanya died as a result of gunfire from a National Guard tank stationed in front of her house at 1756 W. Euclid. Guardsmen claim that they were responding to sniper fire from the second floor, where Tanya lived with her family. They claim to have seen a flash in the window and therefore opened fire on the apartment complex. That flash was actually the flick of [a] match in the dark room, as one of Tanya's male relatives attempted to light a cigarette. Sergeant Mortimer Leblanc of Roseville reportedly fired the first

shot at the apartment complex. The result was that a 50-caliber bullet tore through Tanya's chest. Nobody was held criminally responsible for this child's death.

William N. Dalton, a 19-year-old African American male, died 7/26/67 at 12:45 A.M. Dalton, a high school dropout and ex Job Corps trainee, was known for his singing ability and affectionately called "Willie" by his mother. Walking the streets after 9:30 P.M., Dalton was accused by the police of being a curfew violator. At this point, he was allegedly marched for a few feet, shoved against a wall, and told to run if he wanted. He refused to run. A policeman fired a shot into Willie, from close range. The police report claimed that he was an arsonist and was attempting to flee from the police. When instructed to halt, he kept moving and was shot. The police report lists his death as a "Justifiable Homicide."

Pallbearers carry the casket of four-year-old Tanya Blanding during her funeral on August 1, 1967. Tanya was the youngest victim of the Detroit riots. No one has ever been held responsible for her death. (© AP Images.)

Helen Hall, a 51-year-old white female, died on 7/26/67 around 1 A.M. Mrs. Hall, a native of Illinois, was visiting Detroit on business. The police report claims she was shot by a sniper while staying at the Harlan House Motel on 6500 John C. Lodge Highway. Her friend, Miss Poirier, barely escaped death as the bullets sailed over their heads. Other sources claim that evidence suggests she could have been accidentally shot by a National Guardsman. No one was ever arrested for her death.

Larry Post [was] shot 7/26/67 around 1 A.M. Post was a Sergeant in the National Guard who had a keen interest in cars. Larry was on duty on Wednesday July 26 at a checkpoint area on Dexter. He observed a car occupied with three white males approaching and ordered them to stop, firing his weapon in the air. The order was ignored, the car accelerated, and shots were fired by the other Guardsmen on duty. After the exchange, Post was found wounded with a gunshot to the stomach. He succumbed to his injuries and died at the Henry Ford Hospital on August 9, 1967. His assailants according to [the] police report were listed as "unknown." However, another source claimed one of the men was captured and beaten in police custody.

Aubrey Pollard, a 19-year-old African American male, died 7/26/67. Pollard, who was originally from Oregon, met his demise at the Algiers motel, sometime around 2 A.M. The Algiers Motel, located at 8301 Woodward Avenue, was known as a haven for illicit activities. Pollard and his two friends were allegedly enjoying the company of two white females in a room at the motel. They were playing games and music. They apparently were having a good time until around midnight [when] a group of policemen and National Guardsmen stormed the hotel room in search of snipers. Pollard and his friends were fatally shot and the white girls beaten. Patrolman Ronald August was officially charged with Pollard's death.

Carl Cooper, a 17-year-old African American male, died 7/26/67 around 2 A.M. Cooper was a former spot welder who liked to swim, wear fancy clothes and was extremely lucky at games of chance. He was in the company of Aubrey Pollard and Fred Temple and two white females at the shadowy Algiers Motel. . . . No weapons were found at the scene. The police report lists Cooper's killers as "unknown."

Fred Temple, an 18-year-old African American male, died 7/26/67 around 2 P.M. Temple was an aspiring musician who was in the company of Carl Cooper and Aubrey Pollard in the Algiers Motel at the time of his death. . . . Patrolman Robert Paille was charged with Temple's murder. Paille was eventually acquitted due to the lack of evidence.

George Tolbert, a 20-year-old African American male, was shot 7/26/67 around 5:30 P.M. Tolbert made his living as a TV repairman. Tolbert was walking down the street past a National Guard checkpoint at Dunedin and LaSalle when a bullet fired by a Guardsman hit him. The bullet passed through him and hit his friend who was walking beside him. Tolbert succumbed to his injury ten days later in the hospital. Although he was unarmed and committed no crime, no one was held criminally responsible for his death.

Julius Lawrence Lust, a 26-year-old white male, died 7/26/67 around 9:30 P.M. Lust was one of two white males to be fatally shot during the riots. Lust had a passion for cars. On Wednesday, Lust and his friends decided to steal a car part from a junkyard located at 17130 Joseph Campau, on the fringe of the city. The police came to [the] scene after being alerted by a watchman. Upon seeing the officers, Lust and his companion beat a hasty retreat. Lust was told to stop, but continued to run, and in the process, flashed a shiny object at the policeman.

Thinking that the object was a firearm, the policeman opened fire. The object turned out to be a wrench.

Albert Robinson, a 38-year-old African American male, was shot by National Guardsmen on 7/26/67 around 9:30 P.M. Robinson, a former member of the National Guard, lived in an apartment building at 13318 LaSalle from which police claim snipers were firing. The police report claims the Guardsmen came under fire from snipers and returned fire. At the end of the exchange, Robinson came out of the building bleeding and collapsed. Other sources claim that the Guardsmen entered the building and Robinson attempted to grab a Guardsman's weapon, which then discharged. Robinson died on August 5, 1967, at Detroit General Hospital. . . .

Ernest Rocquemore, an unarmed 19-year-old African American male, was shot outside his home at 3484 St. Jean by a US army paratrooper who had recently returned from service in Vietnam. This shooting occurred as Army troops and police officers were conducting a joint raid in search of looted merchandise—one day after the riot had officially been declared over. The police report suggests that Mr. Rocquemore and several companions sought to flee from the building and were ordered to halt. When one of these persons allegedly brandished "a chrome revolver," the paratrooper fired. Ernest was hit in the back by the shotgun blast and was declared dead on arrival at Detroit General Hospital. The "chrome revolver" mentioned in the police report was, according to several eyewitnesses, actually a transistor radio.

CHAPTER 2

Controversies Surrounding the 1967 Detroit Riots

The Detroit Riots Show the Need for Elected Urban Black Leadership

John W. Smith and Lois H. Smith

Photo on previous page: Michigan National Guardsmen wielding fixed bayonets push back rioters in July 1967. The deployment of the National Guard was very controversial and many of the deaths were attributed to them. (© **Bettmann/Corbis.**)

In the following viewpoint, a professor and a lawyer argue that African Americans in the United States are proportionally under-represented in elected leadership roles. They argue that African Americans must have their own representation, because, they say, white representatives have historically not been responsive to the black community. The authors argue that the black leadership must not only be elected to positions of power, but must also be seen as worthy of respect from its constituents if it is to be able to defuse violent outbreaks. The authors say that developing such a leadership may take some time. John W. Smith was an assistant professor of political science at Indiana University of Pennsylvania; Lois H. Smith was a lawyer in Michigan.

SOURCE. John W. Smith and Lois H. Smith, "First Amendment Freedoms and the Politics of Mass Participation," *Riot in the Cities: An Analytical Symposium on the Causes and Effects,* Richard A. Chikota and Michael C. Moran, eds. Teaneck, NJ: Fairleigh Dickinson University Press, 1970, pp. 67–72. Copyright © 1970 by Fairleigh Dickinson University Press. All rights reserved. Reproduced by permission.

Both a legal and political analysis of the Detroit riot have led us to a dominant observation: *it concerns the role of Negro leadership*. One of the most dramatic moments of the five day period occurred on the first day, Sunday morning, July 23. Negro Democratic Representative John Conyers spoke to a milling crowd on 12th Street. With a bullhorn Conyers said to the crowd "Take it easy brother, I assure you we are in touch with the police. Please disperse. . . ." According to a very perceptive eye-witness account, Conyers moved to the top of a parked vehicle and spoke further, but was forced to stop as rioters broke bottles on the curb and rocks flew around him.

Difficulties of Black Leadership

Fellow Negro Democratic Congressman [Charles] Diggs, from another Detroit District, was no more successful in pacifying the crowds. Negro Hubert Locke, at the time on leave from Wayne State University and acting as an Administrative Assistant to the Police Chief, could do nothing either with the ignited throng.

Why couldn't these three highly placed Negro public officials, two of whom were elected a year before, do anything to snap a quiet victory from the jaws of the riot? Timing alone made rational dialogue that Sunday morning and noon improbable. But even before that day Negro leaders had not been conspicuously successful in constructively organizing as a political minority group so as to present their grievances through conventional political channels.

> Although Negroes account for approximately eleven percent of the total population, they only constitute approximately one percent of Congress.

In fact, throughout the United States, Negro leadership is not proportionately as successful as its white counterpart. Although Negroes account for approximately eleven percent of the total population, they only constitute approximately one percent of Congress. Negroes as a race are therefore underrepresented over ten times their proportionate number in Congress. The Supreme Court may have said that there should be one man, one vote as nearly as practicable, but this doctrine applies to all citizens by area, not to all groups by race.

Until the 1967 off-year campaigns the same disproportionate underrepresentation was true for mayoral positions. Presently Washington, D.C. has an appointed Negro mayor while Cleveland, Ohio along with Gary, Indiana and Flint, Michigan have elected Negro mayors.

All these Congressional and mayoral positions are in the North and only one of the prominently elected Negroes is a Republican, *viz.* Senator [Edward] Brooke of Massachusetts. The deep South still has not produced a state-wide elected Negro official. Mississippi, for example, with 43 percent of its population Negro, the highest concentration in the nation, has one Negro, Robert Clark, in the Jackson Legislature. And his election was unsuccessfully challenged January 2, 1968, just as Julian Bond's position was in the Georgia State Legislature.

Leadership Is Needed

North or South, this chasm of elected Negro leadership is only partially due to discrimination in registering and voting. Negroes as a group lack the educated leadership of skillful wordsmiths who can organize and appeal to the mass citizenry, white as well as black. And it is quality leadership more than any of a host of other factors which the Negroes need to develop for their race. Leadership is the *sine qua non* [essential ingredient] of politics, more important than numbers, more potent than ideas, more effective than access, more valuable even than money. Leadership alone can orchestrate an organization, recruit members, clarify a blaring but unscored idea, create access, and produce wealth.

Negroes no longer accept white leadership: black pride requires black leaders. The NAACP [National Association for the Advancement of Colored People] may have been founded by Caucasians, but the association will surely not now be led by them. SNCC [Student Nonviolent Coordinating Committee] has also evolved, in this case from Christian biracial origins in 1960 into an exclusively secular Negro group. Saul Alinski [a community organizer and writer] may be a consultant to Negro urban ghetto dwellers, but he cannot and does not aspire daily to lead them.

Democracy is postulated on the assumption people and groups will look out for their own welfare; self-help is self-rule. That is why three commentators can judge the riots as ultimately a positive sign. The entelechy or vital force directing the life of a democracy is control over one's destiny. In turn group assertiveness is the

Congressman John Conyers tried unsuccessfully to disperse the rioters on July 23, 1967. (© **AP Images.**)

The Political Career of John Conyers

Congressman John Conyers Jr. was born in Detroit to John and Lucille Conyers. . . . In October 1961 Conyers was appointed by Gov. John B. Swainson to be a referee for the Workman's Compensation Department. When redistricting created a second black-majority congressional district in Detroit in 1964, Conyers entered the race. Running on a platform of "Equality, Jobs, and Peace," he won his first election by a mere 108 votes and became the second black to serve as congress representative from Michigan. . . . In subsequent years, Conyers gained reelection by ever increasing margins, winning his fifteenth term, in 1992, with 84 percent of the vote.

In his long tenure as representative of Michigan's First District, and as a founding member of the Congressional Black Caucus (CBC), Conyers has worked to promote social welfare and civil rights causes. Soon after his arrival in Washington, he supported President Lyndon Johnson's Medicare program and the Voting Rights Act (1965). Just four days after the assassination of the Rev. Dr. Martin Luther King Jr. in April 1968, Conyers submitted a bill to create a national holiday on the birthday of the slain civil rights leader. Getting federal approval for the holiday proved to be an arduous task; fifteen years passed before President Ronald Reagan signed the bill into law on November 22, 1983. In the interim, Conyers had convinced a number of mayors and governors throughout the country to declare January 15 a local or state holiday.

While Conyers has advocated independent black political movements, he has avoided aligning himself with black

condition upon which the group basis of politics rests, that collectivities wishing recognition seek that recognition. Negroes are beginning to take their destiny into their own hands, albeit with the wrong tools. The point to be emphasized is Negro desire for recognition, not the present Negro tools for demanding that recognition. The goal is praiseworthy, the procedure is galling.

African Americans Must Organize

But, you will object, Negroes need not be recognized as a group, but as individuals. This is true, and this is the separatists. At the National Black Political Convention held in Gary, Indiana, in March 1972, Conyers was critical of those who advocated forming an independent black political party, saying, "I don't think it is feasible to go outside the two-party system. I don't know how many of us blacks could be elected without white support."

During the 1980s Conyers was often an opponent of the administrations of Ronald Reagan and George H.W. Bush. He spoke out against Bush's efforts to keep Haitian refugees from entering the United States in 1992 and opposed the appointment of conservative African American Clarence Thomas to the Supreme Court. While a lifelong Democrat, Conyers was also at times critical of President Jimmy Carter, as he was when Carter dismissed UN ambassador Andrew Young. In fact, relations between Carter—who had also failed to support the King holiday bill—and Conyers grew so strained that the congressman launched a "dump Jimmy Carter for President" campaign on the eve of the 1980 primaries.

Conyers has served as chairman of the Government Operations Committee and has also served on the House Small Business Committee and the Speaker's Task Force on Minority Set-Asides. In 1998, as the ranking Democrat on the Judiciary Committee, Conyers was a vocal opponent of the impeachment of President Bill Clinton. As of 2011, he is the second longest-serving incumbent in the House.

SOURCE: Christine Lunardini, "John Conyers," Encyclopedia of African-American Culture and History. *New York: Gale, 2006.*

eventual goal of an individualistic community, but if Negroes *qua* Negroes are repressed, then Negroes *qua* Negroes must organize.

But, you will object further, Caucasians will look after Negroes. The United States is a nation of virtual representation. This is not true, however, for such Senators as [segregationist John C.] Stennis of Mississippi. Mississippi Negroes are functionally represented through the NAACP and the factional Freedom Democratic Party, not through the white supremacist Democratic party, or the moribund Republican party. If the Evers brothers[1] do not organize the Negro in Mississippi, who shall pay attention to Negro demands?

In abstract theory, Negroes *per se* need not be elected to office to insure Negroes equal protection of the law. In practice, both racial and ethnic groups develop identification and come to the aid and succor of fellow group members. The test of this, if one is needed, is found among ethnic identifiable members of Congress. Let a Greek-American from North Carolina write Representative [Peter] Kyros of Maine and he will reply, not because the writer is a constituent but because he was a Greek. Again, let a North Dakota Pole write Representative Roman Pucinski of Illinois, and the chances are that solon will answer the correspondence. It all resolves to this: white leadership cannot be a successful surrogate for popularly elected Negro representation because of the nature of pluralistic American group identification and representation.

> Non-elected Negro leaders abound . . . . But non-elected officials do not have political power; at best they have influence.

Non-elected Negro leaders abound: Whitney Young of the Urban League, Roy Wilkins of the NAACP, Ralph Abernathy of the Southern Christian Leadership Conference, Robert Weaver of the Department of Housing and Urban Development, and the Negro businessmen of the Cotillion Club in Detroit and the Detroit Negroes' City—Wide Citizens Action Committee. But non-elected officials do not have political power; at best they have influence. Laws are made by elected legislators and laws are most fully enforced by elected chief administrators. There are proportionately too few Negro elected officials who pass and police the laws. And long ago Negroes learned they could not accept the good will and self-restraint of the whites; they must control their own political destiny.

Perhaps Representative Conyer's near stoning and ridicule by fellow Negroes is an indication that even with popularly elected Negroes tension will not automatically subside. Unless these officials truly represent their fellow members and establish rapport, they may themselves be the target of riots. For example, Flint, Michigan will not be immune to another riot simply because it has a Negro chief administrator. As a larger proportion of the Negro community becomes militant it is possible Negro mainstream politicians may lose their appeal, especially to young male Negroes, and thereby lose the utility of a group-hero in high places. Mr. Conyers, in other words, must not only be a qualified man trained in democratic procedures and nurtured in non-violent political tactics; he must appeal to Negroes who want to identify with him and respect him.

Adequate Representation Will Quell Unrest

In sum, the indispensable key to the potential riotous black urban areas is responsible, popular, elected Negro leadership. The courts *ipso facto* abhor violent actions because of their deep-set major juristic premise that the rule of law is a solution for every conceivable community problem; change can always be peaceful and politically manageable because the procedures for change, the political branches, are always available and run by men of good will. On the other hand, politics in America is deeply set with the premise that when a group is denied access to participate in the conduct of statecraft, it becomes necessary to take to the streets. If a group is not adequately represented and counseled with, and cannot correct the wrong, then it is free to do violence to the system. . . .

> The solution must be . . . the development of a democratically oriented and politically sensitive high quality Negro political leadership.

If it is the group's own fault that it is not participating in the official decision-making processes, then violence may erupt but without that violence being meaningful. The efficient and ultimate escape from this violence is neither judicial punishment of the rioters nor legislative punishment for leaders who use interstate commerce to incite riots. The solution must be positive: it must be the development of a democratically oriented and politically sensitive high quality Negro political leadership.

Development, however, takes time.

Note

1. Medgar and Charles Evers were Mississippi civil rights activists. Medgar was assassinated in 1963 by a white supremacist.

An Elected Urban Black Leadership Did Not Solve Racial Problems in Detroit

Amy Lee and Darren A. Nichols

In the following viewpoint, two journalists report that after the 1967 riots in Detroit, elected leadership in the city shifted to African Americans. However, at the same time this shift occurred, many whites left the city for the suburbs, and power in the region flowed away from the city to white-majority areas. Thus, the authors maintain, the increase in black leadership has not helped black residents as much as some hoped it would. The authors suggest that racial problems still haunt the city, which has impacted Detroit's ongoing economic troubles. Amy Lee and Darren A. Nichols are journalists for the *Detroit News*.

African-Americans have won numerous elected and appointed leadership positions in the 40 years since civil upheaval shook Detroit, from the executive branch of the federal government, to state and judicial offices, to the mayor's offices of several communities across the region.

Lingering Problems

Many of those local victories, however, have come as resources shifted from aging cities to growing suburbs, leaving black leaders with lingering problems.

The rise of black leadership in cities such as Detroit and Pontiac occurred at the same time wealthier residents were seeking larger homes and property in the suburbs, said Eric Foster, director of business and political development for the Urban Consulting Group in Detroit.

> Detroit's shift to African-American leadership after 1967 can be seen as 'a silver lining in a very dark cloud.'

"You really couldn't get into new development. Black politicians were caretakers and given cities that were wrought with infrastructure challenges. They had to basically just maintain," Foster said. "If you started 20 years late in the race, you're always going to be behind. You can't fault those mayors with the disinvestment they had."

Six years after the 1967 Detroit disturbance, Detroiters for the first time elected an African-American mayor in Coleman Young, triggering the city's shift to a majority black power structure from one that had been reserved for whites.

African-Americans Gain Leadership Roles

At the same time African-Americans were rising in prominence in Detroit, politicians in neighboring suburbs, such as the late Dearborn Mayor Orville Hubbard, were building boundaries —trumpeting racial segregation.

Detroit's shift to African-American leadership after 1967 can be seen as "a silver lining in a very dark cloud," said Detroit City Council President Ken Cockrel Jr.

That shift is clearly evident at Detroit's corridors of power: eight of nine council members are African-American, as is Mayor Kwame Kilpatrick and most of his top aides.

Blacks have ascended to increasingly prominent and respected roles:

U.S. Appeals Judge Damon Keith has held powerful and visible roles in Detroit and nationally; he chaired Michigan's Civil Rights Commission in 1967.

Detroit's longtime U.S. Rep. John Conyers Jr., D-Detroit, chairs the House Judiciary Committee.

Kilpatrick's mother, U.S. Rep. Carolyn Cheeks Kilpatrick, D-Detroit, chairs the Congressional Black Caucus and sits on the House Appropriations Committee.

In Metro Detroit, cities such as Inkster in Wayne County and Southfield and Pontiac in Oakland County are led by African-American mayors, and the Oakland County Commission also has elected black representatives.

But in Macomb County, with the lowest black population among the

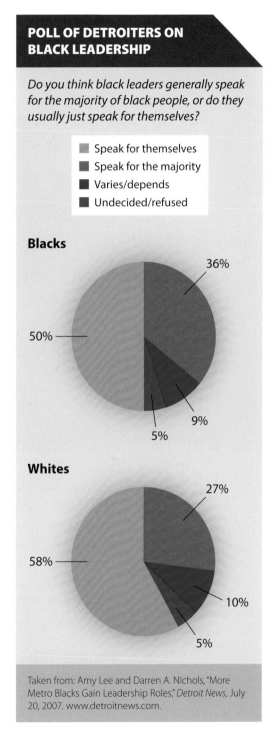

POLL OF DETROITERS ON BLACK LEADERSHIP

Do you think black leaders generally speak for the majority of black people, or do they usually just speak for themselves?

Speak for themselves
Speak for the majority
Varies/depends
Undecided/refused

Blacks

36%
50%
9%
5%

Whites

27%
58%
10%
5%

Taken from: Amy Lee and Darren A. Nichols, "More Metro Blacks Gain Leadership Roles," *Detroit News*, July 20, 2007. www.detroitnews.com.

A historic building in downtown Detroit sits in ruins covered by plants in May 2012. Detroit's ongoing political, social, and economic problems since the end of the 1960s have left thousands of homes and buildings abandoned and taken over by vegetation. (© Julie Dermansky/Corbis.)

region's biggest three counties, none of its 26-member board is a person of color.

"Anyone's who's a first, a first female, a first African American, it opens the door," said Southfield Mayor Brenda Lawrence, who in November 2001 became the city's first African-American mayor.

"It happens," she said, "but sometimes people are leery of stepping out."

Power Moves to the Suburbs

As representation for blacks has grown, however, many contend that the real power has shifted to the suburbs, where three-quarters of the region's residents now live.

Many see the seat of power in Oakland County, where Executive L. Brooks Patterson has been a lightning rod on racial issues since 1971, when he represented a Pontiac mother fighting against busing white students in Pontiac.

"Most Detroiters knew me as the guy on TV who was arguing against busing, and concluded Brooks Patterson is a racist," he said. "It's a bad rap, but I make no apologies."

Both former Detroit Mayor Dennis Archer and Kilpatrick cultivated much warmer relations with Patterson and have fought to protect Detroit institutions from state or regional control.

Kilpatrick, 37 and in his second term as mayor of the nation's 10th largest city, sees irony in the fact that he's charged with tackling political, racial and economic problems that were woven into the fabric of Detroit culture in July 1967, three years before he was born.

"I'm supposed to fix the stuff that went wrong," he said. "People just left, so we never had racial healing. The most important lesson here is that you can . . . destroy your community if you don't seriously sit down and deal with the tension between the races. This has destroyed us economically for 40 years."

The Detroit Riots Showed the Need for More Government Programs in Cities

Report of the National Advisory Commission on Civil Disorders

In the following viewpoint, an investigative commission argues that the United States is in danger of turning into two societies: one white and affluent, one black and disadvantaged. The commission recommends that the government should initiate new programs to address the inequality of inner-city ghettos. These programs, the commission says, should include efforts to address joblessness, poverty, and inequality in the inner city. They should also, according to the commission, be aimed at encouraging integration, so that black people are not left abandoned in inner-city neighborhoods. The National Advisory Commission on Civil Disorders, known as the Kerner Commission, was an eleven-member commission established by President Lyndon B. Johnson to investigate

SOURCE. "Introduction," *Report of the National Advisory Commission on Civil Disorders*, 1968.

the causes of the 1967 race riots in the United States and to provide recommendations.

The summer of 1967 again brought racial disorders to American cities, and with them shock, fear and bewilderment to the nation.

The worst came during a two-week period in July, first in Newark and then in Detroit. Each set off a chain reaction in neighboring communities.

Answering Three Questions

On July 28, 1967, the President of the United States established this Commission and directed us to answer three basic questions:

What happened?

Why did it happen?

What can be done to prevent it from happening again?

To respond to these questions, we have undertaken a broad range of studies and investigations. We have visited the riot cities; we have heard many witnesses; we have sought the counsel of experts across the country.

> Our nation is moving toward two societies, one black, one white—separate and unequal.

This is our basic conclusion: Our nation is moving toward two societies, one black, one white—separate and unequal.

Reaction to last summer's disorders has quickened the movement and deepened the division. Discrimination and segregation have long permeated much of American life; they now threaten the future of every American.

This deepening racial division is not inevitable. The movement apart can be reversed. Choice is still possible.

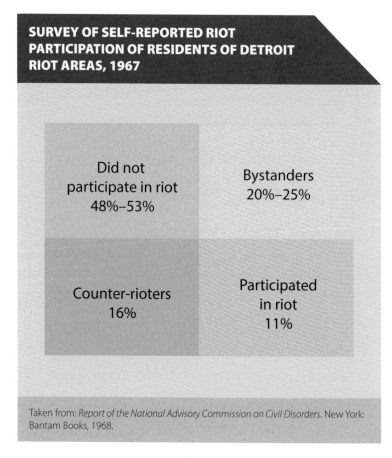

SURVEY OF SELF-REPORTED RIOT PARTICIPATION OF RESIDENTS OF DETROIT RIOT AREAS, 1967

Did not participate in riot
48%–53%

Bystanders
20%–25%

Counter-rioters
16%

Participated in riot
11%

Taken from: *Report of the National Advisory Commission on Civil Disorders*. New York: Bantam Books, 1968.

Our principal task is to define that choice and to press for a national resolution.

To pursue our present course will involve the continuing polarization of the American community and, ultimately, the destruction of basic democratic values.

The alternative is not blind repression or capitulation to lawlessness. It is the realization of common opportunities for all within a single society.

This alternative will require a commitment to national action—compassionate, massive and sustained, backed by the resources of the most powerful and the richest nation on this earth. From every American it will require new attitudes, new understanding, and, above all, new will.

The vital needs of the nation must be met; hard choices must be made, and, if necessary, new taxes enacted.

Violence cannot build a better society. Disruption and disorder nourish repression, not justice. They strike at the freedom of every citizen. The community cannot—it will not—tolerate coercion and mob rule.

Violence and destruction must be ended—in the streets of the ghetto and in the lives of people.

Segregation and poverty have created in the racial ghetto a destructive environment totally unknown to most white Americans.

What white Americans have never fully understood but what the Negro can never forget—is that white society is deeply implicated in the ghetto. White institutions created it, white institutions maintain it, and white society condones it.

It is time now to turn with all the purpose at our command to the major unfinished business of this nation. It is time to adopt strategies for action that will produce quick and visible progress. It is time to make good the promises of American democracy to all citizens—urban and rural, white and black, Spanish-surname, American Indian, and every minority group.

Our recommendations embrace three basic principles:

- To mount programs on a scale equal to the dimension of the problems:
- To aim these programs for high impact in the immediate future in order to close the gap between promise and performance;
- To undertake new initiatives and experiments that can change the system of failure and frustration that now dominates the ghetto and weakens our society.

These programs will require unprecedented levels of funding and performance, but they neither probe deeper nor demand more than the problems which called them forth. There can be no higher priority for national action and no higher claim on the nation's conscience. . . .

Factors That Created a Mood of Violence

In addressing the question "Why did it happen?" we shift our focus from the local to the national scene, from the particular events of the summer of 1967 to the factors within the society at large that created a mood of violence among many urban Negroes.

> Race prejudice has shaped our history decisively; it now threatens to affect our future.

These factors are complex and interacting; they vary significantly in their effect from city to city and from year to year; and the consequences of one disorder, generating new grievances and new demands, become the causes of the next. Thus was created the "thicket of tension, conflicting evidence and extreme opinions" cited by the President.

Despite these complexities, certain fundamental matters are clear. Of these, the most fundamental is the racial attitude and behavior of white Americans toward black Americans.

Race prejudice has shaped our history decisively; it now threatens to affect our future.

White racism is essentially responsible for the explosive mixture which has been accumulating in our cities since the end of World War II. Among the ingredients of this mixture are:

- Pervasive discrimination and segregation in employment, education and housing, which have resulted in the continuing exclusion of great numbers of Negroes from the benefits of economic progress.

- Black in-migration and white exodus, which have produced the massive and growing concentrations of impoverished Negroes in our major cities, creating a growing crisis of deteriorating facilities and services and unmet human needs.

- The black ghettos where segregation and poverty converge on the young to destroy opportunity and enforce failure. Crime, drug addiction, dependency on welfare, and bitterness and resentment against society in general and white society in particular are the result.

At the same time, most whites and some Negroes outside the ghetto have prospered to a degree unparalleled in the history of civilization. Through television and other media, this affluence has been flaunted before the eyes of the Negro poor and the jobless ghetto youth.

Yet these facts alone cannot be said to have caused the disorders. Recently, other powerful ingredients have begun to catalyze the mixture:

- Frustrated hopes are the residue of the unfulfilled expectations aroused by the great judicial and legislative victories of the Civil Rights Movement and the dramatic struggle for equal rights in the South.

- A climate that tends toward approval and encouragement of violence as a form of protest has been created by white terrorism directed against nonviolent protest; by the open defiance of law and federal authority by state and local officials resisting desegregation; and by some protest groups engaging in civil disobedience who turn their backs on nonviolence, go beyond the constitutionally protected rights of petition and free assembly, and resort to violence to attempt to compel alteration of laws and policies with which they disagree.

- The frustrations of powerlessness have led some Negroes to the conviction that there is no effective alternative to violence as a means of achieving redress of grievances, and of "moving the system." These frustrations are reflected in alienation and hostility toward the institutions of law and government and the white society which controls them, and in the reach toward racial consciousness and solidarity reflected in the slogan "Black Power."

- A new mood has sprung up among Negroes, particularly among the young, in which self-esteem and enhanced racial pride are replacing apathy and submission to "the system."

> "Virtually every major episode of violence was foreshadowed by an accumulation of unresolved grievances."

- The police are not merely a "spark" factor. To some Negroes police have come to symbolize white power, white racism and white repression. And the fact is that many police do reflect and express these white attitudes. The atmosphere of hostility and cynicism is reinforced by a widespread belief among Negroes in the existence of police brutality and in a "double standard" of justice and protection—one for Negroes and one for whites. . . .

What Can Be Done?

Our investigation of the 1967 riot cities establishes that virtually every major episode of violence was foreshadowed by an accumulation of unresolved grievances and by widespread dissatisfaction among Negroes with the unwillingness or inability of local government to respond.

Overcoming these conditions is essential for community support of law enforcement and civil order. City governments need new and more vital channels of communication to the residents of the ghetto; they need to improve their capacity to respond effectively to community needs before they become community grievances; and they need to provide opportunity for meaningful involvement of ghetto residents in shaping policies and programs which affect the community.

The Commission recommends that local governments:

- Develop Neighborhood Action Task Forces as joint community government efforts through which more effective communication can be achieved, and the delivery of city services to ghetto residents improved.
- Establish comprehensive grievance-response mechanisms in order to bring all public agencies under public scrutiny.
- Bring the institutions of local government closer to the people they serve by establishing neighborhood

The National Advisory Commission on Civil Disorders, which was convened in the aftermath of the Detroit riots, meets in Washington, DC, in 1968. Among its members were New York City mayor John Lindsay (far left) and Illinois governor Otto Kerner (second from left). (© **Bettmann/ Corbis.**)

outlets for local, state and federal administrative and public service agencies.

- Expand opportunities for ghetto residents to participate in the formulation of public policy and the implementation of programs affecting them through improved political representation, creation of institutional channels for community action, expansion of legal services, and legislative hearings on ghetto problems.

In this effort, city governments will require state and federal support.

The Commission recommends:

- State and federal financial assistance for mayors and city councils to support the research, consultants, staff and other resources needed to respond effectively to federal program initiatives.
- State cooperation in providing municipalities with the jurisdictional tools needed to deal with their problems; a fuller measure of financial aid to urban areas; and the focusing of the interests of suburban communities on the physical, social and cultural environment of the central city.

Improving Relations Between Police and Minority Communities

The abrasive relationship between the police and the minority communities has been a major—and explosive—source of grievance, tension and disorder. The blame must be shared by the total society.

The police are faced with demands for increased protection and service in the ghetto. Yet the aggressive patrol practices thought necessary to meet these demands themselves create tension and hostility. The resulting grievances have been further aggravated by the lack of effective mechanisms for handling complaints against the police. Special programs for bettering police-community relations have been instituted, but these alone are not enough. Police administrators, with the guidance of public officials, and the support of the entire community, must take vigorous action to improve law enforcement and to decrease the potential for disorder.

The Commission recommends that city government and police authorities:

- Review police operations in the ghetto to ensure proper conduct by police officers, and eliminate abrasive practices.

- Provide more adequate police protection to ghetto residents to eliminate their high sense of insecurity, and the belief of many Negro citizens in the existence of a dual standard of law enforcement.

- Establish fair and effective mechanisms for the redress of grievances against the police, and other municipal employees.

- Develop and adopt policy guidelines to assist officers in making critical decisions in areas where police conduct can create tension.

- Develop and use innovative programs to ensure widespread community support for law enforcement.

- Recruit more Negroes into the regular police force, and review promotion policies to ensure fair promotion for Negro officers.

- Establish a "Community Service Officer" [CSO] program to attract ghetto youths between the ages of 17 and 21 to police work. These junior officers would perform duties in ghetto neighborhoods, but would not have full police authority. The federal government should provide support equal to 90 percent of the costs of employing CSOs on the basis of one for every ten regular officers. . . .

The Future of Central Cities Is Grim

By 1985, the Negro population in central cities is expected to increase by 72 percent to approximately 20.8 million. Coupled with the continued exodus of white families to the suburbs, this growth will produce majority Negro populations in many of the nation's largest cities.

The future of these cities, and of their burgeoning Negro populations, is grim. Most new employment opportunities are being created in suburbs and outlying areas. This trend will continue unless important changes in public policy are made.

> We can pursue integration by combining ghetto 'enrichment' with policies which will encourage Negro movement out of central city areas.

In prospect, therefore, is further deterioration of already inadequate municipal tax bases in the face of increasing demands for public services, and continuing unemployment and poverty among the urban Negro population.

Three choices are open to the nation:

- We can maintain present policies, continuing both the proportion of the nation's resources now allocated to programs for the unemployed and the disadvantaged, and the inadequate and failing effort to achieve an integrated society.

- We can adopt a policy of "enrichment" aimed at improving dramatically the quality of ghetto life while abandoning integration as a goal.

- We can pursue integration by combining ghetto "enrichment" with policies which will encourage Negro movement out of central city areas.

The first choice, continuance of present policies, has ominous consequences for our society. The share of the nation's resources now allocated to programs for the disadvantaged is insufficient to arrest the deterioration of life in central city ghettos. Under such conditions, a rising proportion of Negroes may come to see in the deprivation and segregation they experience, a justification for violent protest, or for extending support to now isolated extremists who advocate civil disruption. Large-scale and continuing violence could result, followed by white retaliation, and, ultimately, the separation of the two communities in a garrison state.

Even if violence does not occur, the consequences are unacceptable. Development of a racially integrated society, extraordinarily difficult today, will be virtually impossible when the present black ghetto population of 12.5 million has grown to almost 21 million.

To continue present policies is to make permanent the division of our country into two societies; one, largely Negro and poor, located in the central cities; the other, predominantly white and affluent, located in the suburbs and in outlying areas.

The second choice, ghetto enrichment coupled with abandonment of integration, is also unacceptable. It is another way of choosing a permanently divided country. Moreover, equality cannot be achieved under conditions of nearly complete separation. In a country where the economy, and particularly the resources of employment, are predominantly white, a policy of separation can only relegate Negroes to a permanently inferior economic status.

We believe that the only possible choice for America is the third—a policy which combines ghetto enrichment with programs designed to encourage integration of substantial numbers of Negroes into the society outside the ghetto.

Enrichment must be an important adjunct to integration, for no matter how ambitious or energetic the program, few Negroes now living in central cities can be quickly integrated. In the meantime, large-scale improvement in the quality of ghetto life is essential. . . .

But this can be no more than an interim strategy. Programs must be developed which will permit substantial Negro movement out of the ghettos. The primary goal must be a single society, in which every citizen will be free to live and work according to his capabilities and desires, not his color.

Government Intervention Caused the Detroit Riots

David R. Henderson

In the following viewpoint, a researcher argues that government programs were the cause of the Detroit riots in 1967. The author contends that the police policy of raiding "blind pigs" in Detroit, where black people gathered for drinking and gambling, directly inspired the Detroit riots. He also says that government urban planning policies, whereby old neighborhoods were leveled and rebuilt, had a destructive effect on African American communities and created a scarcity of affordable housing. The author criticizes the national Kerner Commission for recommending more government intervention in the wake of the riots, when it would have been better to call for less police harassment and an end to urban renewal. David R. Henderson is a research fellow with the Hoover Institution and an economics professor at the Graduate School of Business and Public Policy at the Naval Postgraduate School.

SOURCE. David R. Henderson, "Henderson's Iron Law of Government Intervention: The 1967 Detroit Riots," *Freeman*, vol. 61, no. 9, November 2011. www.thefreemanonline.org. Copyright © 2007 by Foundation for Economic Education. All rights reserved. Reproduced by permission.

The more I have studied government policy over the last 40 or so years, the more strongly I have come to believe that whatever problem you name, some government intervention—a tax, a subsidy, a spending program, or a government regulation—was an important cause or, at a minimum, made the problem worse. The evidence for this view is so strong that I think it merits being called Henderson's Iron Law of Government Intervention.

Police Oppression

One instance of this law is the famous, or infamous, Detroit riot of 1967. After the riot various pundits "informed" the public that it had happened because so many of Detroit's black inner-city residents were poor and hopeless. That became the accepted explanation and, to the extent that anyone remembers it, probably still is.

Detroit police arrest a man on July 23, 1967, during the riots. Some critics argue that the local police had a long history of aggressive behavior toward African Americans. (© AP Images/Alvin Quinn.)

But a close look at the record reveals a much more interesting story—of a government's police force oppressing people who simply wanted to live their lives peacefully. This is not to say that the people who rioted bore no responsibility—everyone is responsible for his own actions. However, without the police force's intrusion and without a previous federal program that had destroyed a community, the riot probably would not have occurred. And the evidence for this is hidden in plain sight.

During a five-day period in July 1967, 43 people were killed during the riot in Detroit's inner city. Shortly after that, President Lyndon B. Johnson created the National Advisory Commission on Civil Disorders—the so-called Kerner Commission, named after its head, then-governor of Illinois Otto Kerner. (Kerner was later convicted of having taken a bribe while governor and served time in prison.) The Commission was tasked with determining the causes of that and other riots during the summer of 1967 and with making recommendations to prevent such riots in the future.

Its 1968 Report of the National Advisory Commission on Civil Disorders made a big splash, selling about two million copies. The report stated that black poverty was a big cause of the Detroit riots, and its recommendations for more government jobs and housing programs for inner-city residents were explicitly based on that assumption. These recommendations, plus the charge of white racism, received much of the publicity at the time and are what most people took away from the report. Publishers make a distinction between book buyers and book readers: The latter tends to be a small subset of the former. That distinction seems to apply here. It's too bad that more people didn't actually read the report. The Commission's own account of the details of the Detroit riot tells a story that is fundamentally inconsistent with the Commission's own conclusions and recommendations. Here's the report's first paragraph on Detroit: "On

Saturday evening, July 22, the Detroit Police Department raided five 'blind pigs.' The blind pigs had their origin in prohibition days, and survived as private social clubs. Often, they were after-hours drinking and gambling spots."

Police Raids Triggered the Riot

These "blind pigs" were places that inner-city black people went to be with their friends, to drink, and to gamble; in other words, they were places where people peacefully enjoyed themselves and one another. The police had a policy of raiding these places, presumably because the gambling and the unlicensed alcohol were illegal. The police expected only two dozen people to be at the fifth blind pig, the United Community and Civic League on 12th Street, but instead found 82 people gathered to welcome home two Vietnam veterans. The police proceeded to arrest them. "Some," says the Commission report, "voiced resentment at the police intrusion." Who'd have thunk it? The resentment spread and the riot began.

> The triggering cause of the Detroit riot . . . was the government crackdown on people who were going about their lives peacefully.

In short the triggering cause of the Detroit riot, in which more people were killed than in any other riot that summer, was the government crackdown on people who were going about their lives peacefully. For the rioters the last straw was the government's suppression of peaceful, albeit illegal, black capitalism. Interestingly, in its many pages of recommendations for more government programs, the Commission never suggested that the government should end its policy of preventing black people from peacefully drinking and gambling.

This is par for the course. When a government intervention helps cause a problem, even those people who recognize that the intervention was somewhat to blame

The Impacts of Urban Renewal Projects

To counter growing trends of declining inner cities, the first broad program of urban renewal was initiated in the 1950s. Congress funneled substantial amounts of federal financial aid to cities aimed at eliminating slums and ghettos and replacing them with improved housing and industrial and commercial areas. The Housing Act of 1954 provided "categorical" grants to restore older housing, directing public funds to specifically proposed actions. However, new high-rise housing projects of the 1950s and early 1960s soon represented the worst of black ghetto life.

The lack of success of categorical grants led to the Community Development Act of 1974. The act introduced block grants giving cities greater flexibility to address their specific needs through locally developed renewal plans. Using block grants, cities would purchase slum areas, sometimes exercising eminent domain, to force the sale of private property to the government. The city would then demolish the buildings, clear the lots, and sell the land to private developers, or put it to public use. Housing developments, shopping centers, and office complexes were built in the newly cleared areas.

Although federal law required cities to assist displaced residents and businesses in finding new affordable locations, the dislocations often resulted in economic hardships. Urban renewal essentially became black removal. Cities typically built new public housing away from the renewal areas and traditional work sources while reserving renewal areas for the middle and upper income residents to stimulate economic growth.

The results of federally funded urban renewal programs were mixed. A number of declining downtown areas were economically revitalized by introducing new industrial and commercial developments. Thousands of families found improved urban housing and new schools, parks, hospitals, museums, and libraries were erected in cleared slum areas. In some cases neighborhoods became integrated as a result. Many areas cleared under the federal programs, however, remained vacant. The high-rise low income public housing projects attracted poverty, crime, and disease. Consequently, many housing projects experienced high vacancy rates. Critics of urban renewal policies claimed cities' efforts to attract new business and higher-income residents caused cities that were already established to deteriorate.

SOURCE: *"Urban Renewal,"* Gale Encyclopedia of US Economic History, *Thomas Carson and Mary Bonk, eds. Detroit: Gale, 1999.*

rarely call for an end to, or even a scaling down of, such intervention.

The government's fingerprints show up elsewhere in the Commission's report. Urban renewal "had changed 12th Street [where the riot began] from an integrated community into an almost totally black one," says the report. It tells of another area of the inner city to which the rioting had not spread: "As the rioting waxed and waned, one area of the ghetto remained insulated." The 21,000 residents of a 150-square-block area on the northeast side had previously banded together in the Positive Neighborhood Action Committee (PNAC) and had formed neighborhood block clubs. These block clubs were quickly mobilized to prevent the riot from spreading to this area. "Youngsters," wrote the Commission, "agreeing to stay in the neighborhood, participated in detouring traffic." The result: no riots, no deaths, no injuries, and only two small fires, one of which was set in an empty building.

Urban Renewal Contributed to the Riots

What made this area different was obviously the close-knit community the residents had formed. But why had a community developed there and not elsewhere? The report's authors unwittingly hint at the answer: "Although opposed to urban renewal, they [the PNAC] had agreed to co-sponsor with the Archdiocese of Detroit a housing project to be controlled jointly by the archdiocese and PNAC." In other words, the area that had avoided rioting had also successfully resisted urban renewal, the federal government's program of tearing down urban housing in which poor people lived and replacing it with fewer housing units aimed at a more-upscale market. Economist Martin Anderson, in his 1964 book, *The Federal Bulldozer*, had shown many of the problems with urban renewal. Even some of Anderson's harshest critics at the time admitted that urban renewal could be called "Negro clearance." Indeed, at the time, an even blunter term, also beginning with the letter "n," was used.

But the Kerner Commission, even in the face of its own evidence, refused to admit that urban renewal was a contributing factor to the riots. Indeed, the Commission recommended more urban renewal. The Commission's phrasing is interesting, though, because it admits so much about the sorry history of the program:

> Urban renewal has been an extremely controversial program since its inception. We recognize that in many cities it has demolished more housing than it has erected, and that it has often caused dislocation among disadvantaged groups.
>
> Nevertheless, we believe that a greatly expanded but reoriented urban renewal program is necessary to the health of our cities.

In short the commission's antidote to poison was to increase the dose.

Minority Groups Must Revolt Against Oppression

H. Rap Brown

In the following viewpoint, a black activist encourages African Americans to engage in revolutionary action. He says that the United States has a violent culture, and African Americans have no choice but to use violence to gain their freedom. He says that the Detroit riots of 1967 were a sign of black revolutionary sentiment and argues that such revolutionary movements cannot be stopped. H. Rap Brown was chairman of the Student Nonviolent Coordinating Committee in the 1960s and author of the autobiography *Die N ----- Die!* He is currently serving a life sentence for the 2000 shooting of two Atlanta sheriff's deputies.

SOURCE. H. Rap Brown, "The Third World and the Ghetto," *The Voice of Black America: Major Speeches by Negroes in the United States, 1797–1971*, Philip S. Foner, ed. Copyright © 1972 by Philip Foner. Copyright renewed © 2000 by Laura Foner and Elizabeth Foner Vandepaer. All rights reserved. Reprinted with the permission of Simon and Schuster, Inc.

I cannot talk about "The Third World and the Ghetto," for black people who comprise the ghetto are the Third World. You see, we make up the Third World. And we have to understand the revolution, and it is a revolution that America is about to undergo, before we can relate to the Third World internationally. . . .

Freedom by Any Means Necessary

Black people are saying we're not talking about equality, we're talking about freedom, and we're going to be free by any means necessary. A lot of white people who can be participants of the revolution—participants of the Third World, if they would—became offended because they saw the doors being closed on liberals. Well, we don't need liberals, we need revolutionaries. We cannot afford to sit and talk about politics in the form of legality, politics in the form of the '68 [presidential] elections, that does not address itself to the problems of black people. How can you choose between [Democratic president Lyndon] Johnson and [Republican candidate Ronald] Reagan? [French philosopher Albert] Camus raises a very good point. He says, What better way to enslave a man than to give him the vote and call him free? Black people have never been free. We're still experiencing slave revolt; and you have to understand that, if you choose to be a revolutionary. You see, the movement is not merely a black movement; it is a movement of the dispossessed of America. That includes the Puerto Ricans; that includes the Mexican-Americans; that includes the poor whites; that includes any dispossessed man. But we happen to be the vanguard of that movement because we are the most dispossessed. . . .

> There is no justice in this country for black people. Justice is a joke.

We are not against all wars. We are against some wars. We are in favor of wars of liberation. There is no justice in this country for black people. Justice is a joke. . . . You see, the power structure in America, the man, the police force, the governors serve the ruling class in America as does General [William] Westmoreland [leader of US forces] in Vietnam. The very same thing. So we are members of the Third World. Now you have to understand the key role of black people. The liberation of oppressed people across the world depends upon the liberation of black people in this country. . . . It is not only Lyndon Johnson—he is the most visible—but it's the ruling class of America that the fight must be fought against. You have to understand that Standard Oil or Chase Manhattan Bank is as much an enemy to oppressed people as is Lyndon Johnson. I have a bit of advice to the left. That advice is: Don't get left. Because the revolution is going to go on with or without you. The *National Guardian* [where Brown's speech first appeared] is an invaluable paper to the movement, but we don't need sympathetic journalism, we need revolutionary journalism. You have to see yourself as being a part of that revolution. If you can't see yourself in the context of being John Brown [an anti-slavery radical who helped bring about the US Civil War] then bring me the guns. . . . So your role is not in the black movement, it is not in the American Indian movement. If you're white your role is in Appalachia, your role is with the poor white people. We cannot talk about coalitions. We talk about alliances and we talk about alliances from the position of power. We will not make the same mistake that was made with the Populist movement.[1] Now, if you choose to align with black people it has to be from a position of power. . . . Another reason that the *National Guardian* is invaluable is that the *New York Times* is a weapon against freedom, a weapon against people, and every other journal in America that is published by the top people in America is controlled by the government and is a weapon against people.

There Are Two Choices: Oppressor or Revolutionary

So when you look at the black revolution, the black rebellion, when you see a brother in the streets throwing a Molotov cocktail, he's not out there for his health; he's out there for his freedom. Understand that when America raises the question of law and order, it's very easy for Johnson to raise the question of law and order, because he never talks about justice. So the question really becomes whether you choose to be an oppressor or

A man throws a shoe at riot police on July 23, 1967. The police were often seen as oppressors by African Americans in Detroit, and some community leaders encouraged blacks to fight back. (© **AP Images**.)

a revolutionary. And if you choose to be an oppressor, then you are my enemy—not because you are white, but because you choose to oppress me. We are not an antiwhite movement. We are anti*anybody* who is antiblack. Johnson says every day, If Vietnam don't come 'round, Vietnam will be burnt down. I say that if America don't come 'round, America should be burned down. It's the same thing.

> We are not an antiwhite movement. We are anti*anybody* who is antiblack.

But you have to begin to associate; you have to begin to find your identity in your own movement. I cannot go to Appalachia and talk about developing an alliance with poor whites, because racism is rampant in America. I cannot go to American Indians and talk about organizing American Indians. My role is in the black community. Once these communities are organized then we can talk about alliances and maybe coalitions. But not until then. . . . You see, the hippies are a lesson. These were people who were supposed to inherit. They are rejecting America. They say we reject your barbarism, we reject your decadence. So black people are saying the same thing. But we don't choose to use drugs. We choose to fight. Though the hippies are rejecting society, they are apolitical in the way they are going about it, and so we cannot feel a strong alliance with the hippie movement. . . .

So we must choose who we are going to align with. That's what we were talking about in Chicago. That's what black people talked about at the black conference in Newark. Another thing about the movement at this point, the black movement, is that the black movement is a leaderless movement. I am not the leader of the black movement. I only speak about the temperament of the black community, and only because I have a forum, because there are people who speak about it much better than I do—people in Detroit for example. . . . No one person, no black person in America could have stopped Detroit from burning. So, while the movement is now a leaderless movement, it says it needs an ideology. That's the role of black so-called intellectuals. You must develop an ideology for that movement. If not, then we will become oppressors in the end, because we will fight the other dispossessed. So, therefore, the role of revolutionaries is to make revolution. . . . So when you talk about a third world, you have to understand the role that you play in the third world. You have to understand that you are not to be a missionary. We don't need missionaries, we don't need "images" in the revolution, we need revolutionaries. If you can't give a gun, then give a dollar to somebody who can buy a gun. See, you sit out there and you pretend violence scares you, but you watch TV every night and you can't turn it on for five minutes without seeing somebody shot to death or karate-ed to death. Violence is part of your culture. . . . There's no doubt about it. You gave us violence and this is the only value that black people can use to their advantage to end oppression. . . .

Note

1. The reference is to the fact that blacks who supported the Populist Party in the 1890s discovered to their dismay that white Populists were fundamentally racists and that white Populist leaders were in the forefront of the movement in the South to disenfranchise blacks.

Black Revolutionaries Undermine the Cause They Seek to Represent

Detroit News

In the following viewpoint, a Detroit newspaper argues that advocates of black revolution like H. Rap Brown have very little support among African Americans. However, the paper argues, they do have enough support to cause chaotic rebellions such as those in Detroit. The paper worries that the result of such violence will be a white backlash and a movement against civil rights and equality for black people. The paper warns that if this is the case, the United States will become like South Africa, where blacks are legally second-class citizens, and freedom for all people, white and black is severely restricted. The *Detroit News* is one of the major daily newspapers in the city of Detroit.

As Detroit staggered back to its feet, still clearing its streets of snipers, TV news viewers everywhere saw black nationalist leader H. Rap Brown stage his stark crazy histrionics on the Federal Courthouse steps in Alexandria, Va.

Black Revolutionaries Are a Minority

Brown's performances follow a script which could be almost amusing, were they not in a context so horrible. It's a reverse play on the ancient foot-shuffling, "Yassuh, boss" role, a reflex reaction to whites which uses every known epithet for the white man and fiery threats of fire and doom.

"This is a revolution. They gonna have to kill 22 million of us. We gonna burn America down." Monday night in Cambridge it was, "Don't love him (the white man) to death, shoot him to death."

> The Rap Browns, the Stokely Carmichaels and all the lesser-known black revolutionists do not speak for one in 10,000 Negroes.

As deep as American Negroes' resentments may run over racial injustice, the Rap Browns, the Stokely Carmichaels and all the lesser-known black revolutionists do not speak for one in 10,000 Negroes.

They do not speak for the scruffy youths in the street mob, the me-first looters or the casual arsonists, none of whom cares about their revolutionary "big picture." They do not speak for even the most determined of Negro civil rights leaders who urgently seek an end to injustice through legal and political process, or for the millions of ordinary Negro citizens on whose behalf that struggle is waged.

But they do speak, unhappily, for enough bitter and warped people in each of the nation's large cities to mount the kind of guerilla war Detroit has witnessed.

The number of purposeful, organized terror-minded black revolutionaries is not large. But it does not take

Police officers search suspected looters in Detroit on July 24, 1967. Some critics argue that the rioters were mostly thugs out to loot, not political revolutionaries with genuine grievances. (© Bettmann/Corbis.)

many to break that first window, light those first few fires, or mount a sniping campaign. A handful are capable of pushing mobs into acts of tremendous destructiveness, of paralyzing a city.

"Get Tough" Attitudes Won't Work

The tragedy of it all is not the one Rap Brown predicts. The black racists will not burn down America. They will not force white America into killing "22 million of us."

Long before these things happen, they will have goaded and frightened white America into repressive attitudes and measures which put race relations back where they were 70 years ago—or worse.

The signs are grave. The mood, in Congress and in cities and towns everywhere, is "Get tough!" which on its face means get tough with rioters, but for a frightening number, really means, "Get tough with Negroes and to hell with civil rights."

If it prevails, this mood will mean an end to the communications slowly established between white and black toward righting injustice, an end to the reforms so painfully pieced together toward that end, and it will not matter that millions of Negro citizens had and would have no part in lawlessness and violence.

> " The end of that dreadful road . . . will be an America not burned down, but an America in the image of South Africa. "

Such reversals will feed Negro discontent and increase the tensions and fury of civil disorder. That will in turn feed the deadly spiral of repression which will seem necessary to maintain order.

The end of that dreadful road, if we cannot somehow get off it, will be an America not burned down, but an America in the image of South Africa,[1] an America functioning, even prospering, but with 22 million Negroes in legal chains.

And, as the South African experience shows, it will not only be the black man who loses his civil rights. The measures required to keep 22 million Negroes repressed will curb white freedoms as well.

The black revolutionists can yap that it couldn't be worse; that's how things are now for the black man. Heaven knows, we've a long way to go in America, but that claim is insane. Those who make it have to be liars or madmen.

But they can make it come true if they persist and are not somehow stopped.

Note

1. From the 1940s until the 1990s, apartheid made racial discrimination and inequality the law in South Africa.

The 1967 Riots Led to Detroit's Decline

Debbie Schlussel

In the following viewpoint, a political commentator argues that the Detroit riots of 1967 were instigated by black revolutionary groups like the Black Panthers. The author contends that the revolutionaries succeeded in electing black leaders in Detroit, but they also caused so much lawlessness and chaos that white people fled the city. As a result, she maintains that Detroit has experienced massive economic decline. She also argues that black leadership, such as Mayor Kwame Kilpatrick, has failed to rejuvenate the city and has been responsible for ongoing crime, lawlessness, and corruption. Debbie Schlussel is a conservative radio talk show host, columnist, and attorney.

Forty years ago today, several days of race riots began in Detroit.

On July 23, 1967, Black Panthers [a revolutionary black nationalist organization active from 1966 to

---

1982] and assorted other Black extremists (with White hippies and far-leftists backing and encouraging them) eventually wrote their political epitaphs with it (though their movement unfortunately died a long, slow death—far past its time, if there ever was a time). But they robbed and killed Detroit—and a significant portion of Black America with it.

Black Radicals Drove Whites Out of Detroit

Black Panthers and their radical allies, supported by thousands of Black Detroiters, rioted for days, starting fires and destroying the city. They wanted more power in the city. They wanted a Black Mayor, a Black police chief, a Black city council.

Today, they have all those things. And they have nothing. They won the riots, they lost the war. And 43 people died—no, were murdered—in vain (along with countless others since).

As my Dad says, when the riots began, Gentile, White Detroiters ran out to buy bullets. Jews ran out to buy guns (way too late). But eventu-

> " Black Americans, like White Americans, don't want to live in the crime, failed schools, and other living conditions brought to you by the Detroit riots. "

ally, they all ran out—and away—from Detroit. Today, more than nine out of ten Detroiters are Black. And even Blacks are leaving the Detroit morass faster than Roger Bannister [a famous runner]. The city is losing population by the tens of thousands, every year. Black Americans, like White Americans, don't want to live in the crime, failed schools, and other living conditions brought to you by the Detroit riots. Crime under Detroit's Black police chiefs (the city has had several) is at an all-time high, and Detroit Public Schools, under its Black superintendents and school boards (there have been several of those, too), are at their worst, with

The Downfall of Kwame Kilpatrick

When Kwame Kilpatrick was elected mayor of the city of Detroit in 2002, it was with great expectation that he would clean up the troubled city. He was expected to approach the city's problems with enthusiasm as the youngest elected mayor of any major U.S. city. However, after several major scandals which cost the city millions in payouts and legal fees, it came to light through a series of text messages on a city-owned pager that Kilpatrick had an affair with Christine Beatty, his chief of staff. After denying the affair for months, Kilpatrick faced numerous legal charges and was compelled to resign his post in September of 2008. Kilpatrick began his career as a middle school teacher before serving as a state representative to the Michigan legislature.

SOURCE: *"Kwame Kilpatrick,"* Newsmakers, *vol. 2. Detroit, MI: Gale, 2009.*

record high drop-out rates and numbers of illiterate graduates.

When Black radicals started the riots, they achieved their goal of driving out White Detroiters, but their separatism only isolated them. Unlike every other inner city in America, Detroit is not a tourist destination. It's not a place where suburbanites generally clamor to go to nightclubs and restaurants. It's simply too dangerous.

Ongoing Violence

The violence and destruction of the riots never really went away, just the press coverage of it. Such prominent figures as the son of former Detroit Mayor Dennis

Archer and the daughter of Detroit Tigers/Red Wings owner Mike Ilitch have been mugged.

During the Super Bowl [in 2006] with thousands of FBI and Homeland Security agents roaming around, there were two murders in the vicinity of the temporary bars and restaurants dotting the main drag of Woodward Avenue. I say "temporary" because that's what they were. Despite all the moving around of cranes to make it look like something—anything!—positive was going on in the city, Detroit Super Bowl Committee personnel had to lease out shops, restaurants, and bars on 7-day leases. Any more than that, and they couldn't convince anyone to do business on the normally abandoned streets.

Crime is rampant, the city can't attract a major business, and the banana republicans on the city council

Detroit mayor Kwame Kilpatrick addresses the press after resigning in 2008 as part of plea deal in a criminal case—one of the many legal troubles and corruption scandals that have characterized his political career. His wife, Carlita Kilpatrick, stands next to him. (© AP Images/ Carlos Osorio.)

junta are busy passing resolutions to name a tunnel after [long-serving black congressman] John Conyers, declaring Dubai [in the United Arab Emirates] a sister city of Detroit [an economic arrangement], and maintaining Sanctuary City status for illegal aliens. Monica Conyers (wife of the radical Congressman) is symbolic of the city council. Drunk and in fist fights at bars, she's a mess. And so is her legislative body and the city it governs.

With a pimp daddy mayor, Kwame Kilpatrick, who dresses like a Gangsta and is involved in scandal after scandal, the city is the laughing stock. But, hey, the Mayor made an appearance on "Living Large," a now-cancelled national hip-hop show. Thank you very little. Kilpatrick, whom I like to call Kwame the Kingpin, was suspected in the drive-by shooting of "Strawberry," a stripper who allegedly performed in the Mayoral Manoogian Mansion for "His Honor." He used his 21-bodyguard posse of police officers to serve as his personal harem-recruiter and to ferret him to and from different girlfriends.

These are the people who betrayed Blacks in Detroit, not the Whites who took White flight (followed by Black flight) from the city and gave them free reign to "run" the city . . . and fail magnificently. And, yet, they still blame even this on the White man. Is it any surprise with "leadership" like this that the city is a ruin much used by Director Michael Bay as a set for movies? With the city a ghost town, even at lunchtime, he has a cornucopia of empty, decrepit, vandalized buildings—once grand palaces of business and industry—to choose from. And he doesn't have to deal with much traffic—by foot or car—interrupting his shoots.

Detroit Is Crumbling

Instead, Detroit is a burnt out shell. It is the only inner city in America that has not undergone a revival, a gentrification (even Cleveland—the former "Mistake on the Lake"—was reborn). While some of that can be attributed to recent, never-ending downturns in the auto industry, this is a phenomenon that has metastasized throughout the city, even when Ford, GM, and Chrysler were at their height. Now that they, too, are on the unreclaimable decline, it only helps solidify Detroit's rigor mortis.

Drive down the Lodge Freeway, the main artery from Detroit's Northwest suburbs into the city, and you will see burnt out house after burnt out house dotting the freeway. All of them are in Detroit, and all of them—in their burnt out "splendor"—have sat vacant and ashen for years.

Ten years ago, when I was sworn in to practice [law] before U.S. District Court, my father took me to lunch. We walked down the streets of downtown Detroit on a beautiful spring day, but there was hardly a soul as far as the eye could see. Ten years later, nothing has changed. It's only gotten worse.

> Detroit is in the worst condition of any major city in America, except perhaps New Orleans, and that took a hurricane.

Detroit is in the worst condition of any major city in America, except perhaps New Orleans, and that took a hurricane, an act of G-d. Three weeks ago, A&P-owned Farmer Jack—the last national supermarket in Detroit, the last large national retailer in the city—closed its doors and said Sayonara to the environs South of Eight Mile.

This is the legacy of the Detroit riots. And despite all the Detroit newspaper and media hype that those days are over, their legacy has only just begun. To the last Black Panther leaving Detroit: Don't forget to turn out the lights. And start your usual fires, in their place.

[Terrorist leader] Osama Bin Laden has a better chance of getting elected President than Detroit has of arising from the dead. As Mark Twain might say, reports of its rebirth are highly exaggerated.

The 1967 Riots Did Not Cause Detroit's Decline

Don Keko

In the following viewpoint, a secondary school teacher argues that the decline of Detroit did not begin with the riots of 1967. Instead, he argues that people began to leave inner-city Detroit in the 1950s, following the development of the Interstate Highway System. The author says that the highway system made it possible for people to live in the suburbs and commute to work. He adds that African Americans were prevented from moving to the suburbs by racist housing practices. He maintains that the Detroit riots increased tensions between blacks and whites, but the process that led to the decline of Detroit was already well underway by 1967. Don Keko is a history teacher in Flint, Michigan.

M any publications have taken a look at Detroit's decline recently. They make important points. The 1967 riots caused "white flight" from the city. The unions and Big Three [automakers] entered

---

into contracts with expensive legacy costs. America shed its industrial base. Mayor Coleman Young left a Chicago-style legacy of corruption. Over a decade after Young's departure corruption, incompetence, and unemployment have continued to blight Detroit. The '67 riots provide researchers with a convenient starting point for this decline. However, the population decline began a decade earlier. In the fifties, the government created the interstate highway system. Highways made America mobile and people left the cities for the suburbs. People left Detroit for greener pastures and took their money with them.

The Highway System Led to Detroit's Demise

The Interstate Highway Act of 1956 created modern America and provided the hole in the dike that led to Detroit's depopulation and decline. Detroit lobbied hard for a highway system to promote car ownership. Americans could only go so far without roads. The new system would open up the country. Americans could travel everywhere in their automobiles. This new freedom would mean more profits for the auto industry. Consumers would feel the need to purchase vehicles as status symbols and for the freedom of mobility the highways created.

Opening the nation to car travel also opened areas outside the major cities for settlement. People could go to work in the city and live in the suburbs or country. Americans did not have to live in apartments in crowded, dirty cities. Instead, they could live in homes they themselves owned in clean surroundings. There would be elbow room, privacy, and backyard barbeques. This especially appealed to those parents responsible for the baby boom [following World War II]. Many Detroiters began moving to cleaner suburban pastures.

In 1950, Detroit's population stood at 1.8 million. Over the course of the decade, it dropped 10%. On the

The interstate highways built beginning in the 1950s segmented Detroit, further segregated African Americans, and destroyed some of their neighborhoods. (© **Charles E. Rotkin/ Corbis.**)

other hand, the Metro Detroit Region which includes the suburbs surrounding the city grew by 25%. The middle class was abandoning the city a decade or so before the riots. These were auto workers benefiting from the Big Three's halcyon days. High wages, good benefits, and a strong union made the Detroit area a great place to live. Workers took their wages to the suburbs and purchased homes. People could commute between homes in the suburbs and jobs in the city. Meanwhile, the tax base began to decline.

Detroit's Population Declines

The 1967 riots accelerated the exodus. The riots pitted whites against blacks. African-Americans felt besieged by white racism and rebelled. In the aftermath, whites felt besieged by black racism. With highways available to evacuate the populace, whites began to flee the city. African Americans with the resources to move were barred from moving to the suburbs by de facto segregation. During the seventies, Detroit's population declined by over 20%. By 1980, the destruction of Detroit was complete. Despite efforts at revitalization in the nineties, the process has accelerated in recent years.

> Detroit's demise . . . began because people wanted their own homes on their own plots of land.

Detroit's demise did not begin with racial issues in the aftermath of the riots. It did not begin with economic stagnation or the shipping of jobs overseas. It did not begin because of bad deals cut between the UAW [United Auto Workers union] and [automakers] G.M., Ford, and Chrysler. Instead, it began because people wanted their own homes on their own plots of land. The Interstate Highway System gave us Modern America. It created soccer moms, minivans, and the world of *Leave it to Beaver* [a 1950s television sitcom]. However, it also opened a Pandora's Box which began the decline of America's fourth largest city.

The Detroit Riots Hold Lessons for Understanding the 2011 UK Riots

Gary Younge

In the following viewpoint, a journalist discusses the Detroit riots of 1967 in comparison to a large wave of riots in England during August 2011. The author says that researchers found the 1967 rioting was not related directly to economic distress or poverty. Similarly, the riots were not simply the work of riffraff, but, according to the author, were widely regarded as partially justified, even by those in the city who did not participate. He says that the 1967 riots were the result of frustration and of the rising expectations caused by the civil rights movement, which despite some political advances, failed to improve African Americans' lives in Detroit. He suggests a parallel with frustrated expectations among rioters in England. Gary Younge is a feature writer and columnist for the British newspaper the *Guardian*.

Early in the morning on Sunday 23 July 1967 the Detroit police raided an after-hours drinking establishment where more than 80 black men and women were celebrating the return of two Vietnam veterans. This in itself was hardly rare. Police used to raid "blind pigs" all the time.

Causes of the Detroit Riots

What was extraordinary was what came next: an outpouring of protest, violence, looting, police brutality and, ultimately, full-scale federal military intervention. "To live in America, until recently, meant to be far from war," says Calliope Stephanides, the protagonist in Jeffrey Eugenides's novel *Middlesex*, which is set in the city at the time. "Wars happened in south-east Asian jungles . . . But then why, peeking out of the dormer window, did I see a tank rolling by our front lawn?"

Before the week was out there were 43 dead, 467 injured, more than 7,200 arrests, and more than 2,000 buildings destroyed: the deadliest riots in US history.

Nathan Caplan, a psychology professor at the University of Michigan's institute for social research (ISR), was unconvinced by his colleagues' claims that the riots were simply an expression of immaturity and social deviancy. So he went to the affected neighbourhoods with one of his graduate students to conduct some field research.

"There was still smoke in the air and bullets flying when we got there," recalls Caplan. "My academic colleagues had a habit of interpreting reality as though it's just a special case within theory. God forbid that anything they did became useful or that they actually spoke to anybody."

At the same time, Philip Meyer, a national correspondent for Knight Newspapers, which owned the *Detroit Free Press*, was also trying to break out of the constraints of his discipline. Just a few weeks earlier Meyer had returned from a career break as a Nieman fellow at Harvard, where he had studied social research methods.

"Politicians were using them and I felt journalists had to understand them too," he explains.

When the riots in Detroit started he saw an opportunity to apply academic rigour to journalistic reportage. "It struck me like a bolt of lightning," says Meyer. "The University of California had just released their report into the Watts riots and I thought, we could do this too. But people wouldn't have to wait two years for the results. With journalists we could do it faster."

And so they did. Caplan and Meyer got together, drafted a questionnaire and then trained 30 black interviewers to go into the affected areas and gather information. The next week the interviewers went into the field, sending each day's interviews back to the university. In the third week Meyer and Caplan analysed the data and Meyer started writing it up. Just a month after the disturbances had started, the *Free Press* published its findings.

Entitled *The People Beyond 12th street: A Survey of Attitudes of Detroit Negroes After the Riot of 1967*, the report's methodology and language are very much of their time.

Seeking to explain black Detroit to white America, it reads like an anthropological survey of a foreign land.

> There was no correlation between economic status or educational levels and propensity to riot.

"In their alienation the rioters display some similarity to hippies," reads one part. "Both feel that the world is wrong and they want to set themselves apart from it. But hippies accept their share of the world's guilt while rioters project it. The hippie hands you a flower and says: 'Peace.' The rioter shouts: 'Get whitey' and throws a rock."

Nonetheless, even though by modern standards the sample was small and only a minority of those they spoke to were rioters, its data was revelatory.

It showed that, contrary to popular belief, there was no correlation between economic status or educational

levels and propensity to riot. Nor had the riots been the work of recent immigrants from the south. The main grievances were police brutality, overcrowded living conditions, poor housing and lack of jobs.

Linking the Detroit and England Riots

There are relatively few similarities between the Detroit riots in 1967 and those in England last month [August 2011, when towns across England experienced widespread rioting, looting, and arson]. The unrest in Detroit was part of a national conflagration led largely by the young. A riot had ended in Newark a week before and would continue in Milwaukee and Washington DC just days after. But these disturbances were rooted in racial conflict. "Detroit was becoming increasingly black and the police force and the city government remained primarily white," explains the veteran Detroit activist and author Grace Lee Boggs. "So the institutions in the city were seen as occupation forces."

It was also a pivotal moment in American racial history. A period of mass activism in the south had produced civil rights legislation just a few years before, securing black Americans the right to equality and the vote. 1967 was the year [boxer] Muhammad Ali refused to serve in Vietnam, Cleveland became the first major city to elect a black mayor and bans on mixed-race marriages were finally made unconstitutional.

But while the contexts in England in 2011 and in Detroit more than 40 years earlier were quite different, many of the most popular explanations for the root causes were startlingly similar. The youth of those involved and the looting led many to dismiss those involved as just riffraff running amok.

"I was hearing that the riots were the product of immaturity and social deviancy by the lumpenproletariat [the underclass]," recalls Caplan. "But that's not what we were finding."

Then there is the apparent disconnect between the event that triggered the riot and the prevailing conditions that might explain it. "Every riot has a precipitating event," explains Meyer. "But then there are always more subtle factors."

Indeed, thanks largely to union jobs at the city's car plants, African Americans were materially better off in Detroit than elsewhere in the country. More than 40% owned their own homes. The city had the largest chapter of the NAACP [National Association for the Advancement of Colored People], the nation's oldest and largest civil rights organization in the country and was the only city with two black congressmen.

By revealing there was no link between income or education levels and rioters, and that those born in Detroit were three times more likely to have been involved than those from the south, the ISR/*Detroit Free Press* survey provided evidence that effectively countered popular misconceptions. "The riffraff theory and the southern migrant theory just stopped being propagated," says Meyer. "They were more likely to be young but that's because they had less to lose. In that sense the young were like leading edge consumers."

"It gave an empirical basis to address some interpretations and it put them straight into the public sphere," says Caplan.

It also gave voice to the complex attitudes towards social unrest in areas most likely to play host to them. The overwhelming majority of black people in Detroit at the time (84%) thought the riots could happen again. Only a quarter believed they had more to gain than lose by resorting to violence. But, explained Meyer at the time, "even those who think the long-term effects of violence are likely to be bad see some compensating benefits." "They know we mean business now," one 31-year-old told him.

The Kerner Commission set up by the president, Lyndon Johnson, to examine the cause of the riots in Detroit and elsewhere, used the data from the *Detroit Free Press*/ISR survey in reaching its findings. "What white Americans have never fully understood—but what the Negro can never forget—is that white society is deeply implicated in the ghetto," it argued. "White institutions created it, white institutions maintain it, and white society condones it." Famously it concluded: "Our nation is moving towards two societies, one black, one white—separate and unequal."

(© **"Would You Like to Catch a Play Tonight or Stay at Home and Watch the Riots on TV?,"** cartoon by Lindsay Foyle. www .CartoonStock.com.)

Long-Term Effects of the Detroit Riots

You can certainly see that society in Detroit today. Most respondents to the survey believed the attitudes of whites towards blacks would improve over the following five years. In fact whites just left the city en masse for the suburbs; a few decades later more affluent blacks followed. Following the collapse of the US car industry a couple of decades later, Detroit might best be described as post-industrial. But the immediate impression is post-apocalyptic: empty lots, abandoned houses, multistorey buildings left derelict, entire blocks boarded up. Detroit has lost 25% of its population in the past 10 years. It's what you would imagine a city would look like when capitalism decides that it doesn't really need the people any more.

Five minutes from 12th Street (which has been renamed Rosa Parks Boulevard) and Clairmount, the intersection where the riot started, you can buy a house for $1200 (£750). The only ad on the side of a row of dilapidated storefronts is for criminal defence lawyers. And even that has been defaced.

So if poverty and poor education did not cause the riots, what did? Alongside police brutality, Boggs describes an alienated youth who saw that technological changes in manufacturing would make them economically obsolete. "Young people felt expendable. They had to make a way out of no way."

The former Black Panther Wayne Curtis suggests that the apparent wealth belied lives of discrimination. "Growing up we saw people riding around in Cadillac convertibles. But we didn't see the conditions they worked in and the racism in the factories. They still had to deal with the police. We just didn't understand how marginalised they were."

Curtis recalls thinking that the civil rights victories had settled the question of equality once and for all. "We were told that this was it; that if we could vote everything would be OK. But it took a while to understand how the power structure works."

Both Caplan and Meyer call this the problem of rising expectations. Having fought for and ostensibly won social equality, African Americans found that did not translate into economic justice. "Young black kids just weren't getting jobs," says Caplan. "The opportunity structure was just too narrow and everyone knew it. So you would see young people breaking windows and looting stores. But it was the older ones who were more frustrated and more militant in their views."

> "Having fought for and ostensibly won social equality, African Americans found that did not translate into economic justice."

CHAPTER 3
Personal Narratives

A Journalist Who Lived in the Riot Zone Reports on Her Experiences

Sandra A. West

In the following viewpoint, a resident of Detroit describes her fear during the days of rioting and arson in 1967. She talks about her worry that her house would be set on fire by sparks, and her terror at gunshots near her home. She saw looters throughout the neighborhood, including some as young as eight or nine. She maintains that many in the neighborhood believed that the chief rioters came from outside of Detroit. She suggests that they instigated the violence and looting and then left, leaving those in the neighborhood to deal with the fallout. Sandra A. West was a staff reporter for United Press International and a longtime Detroit resident.

By 5 P.M. Sunday night it was necessary to close our home to keep the smoke from saturating the house.

At 6:30 P.M. the electricity went out. We couldn't use our electric fan and we were forced to open the house again.

Raging fires burned out of control for blocks and blocks.

Thick black smoke and cinders rained down so heavily they blocked the view to homes as close as 20 feet.

Families Prepare for the Worst

Friends of ours set up telephone relay systems to pass on any new information. Rumors spread as fast as the blazes and it was hard to know what was true.

Some of the families on the blocks between 12th and Linwood Ave. packed their belongings and prepared to leave during the night if it became necessary. We were one of those families.

Several homes caught fire from the burning stores.

> Fire had destroyed their home. Tears streamed down the mother's face.

A man, his wife and two small children stumbled along the street with a suitcase and a bedsheet filled with the few belongings they could grab. Fire had destroyed their home. Tears streamed down the mother's face.

Neighbors sat up on their porches all night. We rummaged around for candles and flashlights.

Looters drove pickup trucks loaded with everything from floor mops to furniture. Price tags still dangled from the merchandise. Youngsters no more than 8 or 9 years old rode two on a bicycle with loot stuffed inside their shirts and clutched under their arms.

A 12-year-old boy flashed a diamond ring. He said he found it on his lawn.

A bayonet sticks out of a National Guard truck patrolling the west side of Detroit in July 1967. Interactions with the National Guard traumatized many people who lived through the riots. (© **Corbis.**)

We walked to 12th St. where the riot began. We watched as arsonists touched off fires at two establishments within a block.

Burglar alarms wailed. They went unanswered.

Negro-owned stores had hastily printed signs reading, "Soul Brother."

I have lived in the area since 1954. Sunday I saw sights I never dreamed possible.

Fires, Looters, and Gunfire

At one point during the long two days, my neighborhood, near the center of Detroit's rioting and looting, held me prisoner. Bullets snapped around my house.

The burning, the choking on heavy smoke, the fear that my home would be set ablaze by flying cinders, the looting, the harassment from looters who tore through my yard daring me with their stares to order them off my property, the armed police, state police and National Guardsmen who glared and pointed their guns at me as they cruised the neighborhood—all were surpassed when the sound of gunshots riddled the night.

> The out-of-towners . . . kept [the riot] going and have now returned to their home towns loaded down with riches from Detroit.

Snipers had apparently set up sites on a nearby street and were shooting it out with Guardsmen. Miraculously no bullets hit the house.

The feeling is growing in my neighborhood that the riot was instigated by out-of-town forces.

The out-of-towners did not actually start the riot, they kept it going and have now returned to their home towns loaded down with riches from Detroit and "leaving us with nothing but destruction."

"An old rattle-trap Chevy came tearing down the street at about 10 o'clock Sunday morning," a neighbor told me. "There were two young men inside . . . that car had New York plates."

A great many of the cars I saw cruising the area during the height of the looting Sunday had Ohio and Illinois license plates.

My next door neighbor, who is white, came out of his house briefly Tuesday to empty the garbage. I had not seen him since Sunday.

A Resident of the Detroit Suburbs Remembers the Riots

Jeff L. Howe

In the following viewpoint, a Detroit suburb resident remembers his experience as a sixteen-year-old during the riots of 1967. At the time, the author was living in Walled Lake, Michigan, a rural suburb about forty miles northwest of Detroit. He says that people in the suburbs were nervous about the rioting in Detroit. Then, he says, a rumor started that blacks from Detroit were advancing on Walled Lake. Families took out shotguns, hid daughters in the basement, and got ready to defend their homes. The author maintains that all this preparation was completely unnecessary; the rioting never came anywhere near Walled Lake. The panic, he says, was caused by anger, fear, and misinformation. Jeff L. Howe is a writer, musician, and amateur geologist.

SOURCE. Jeff L. Howe, "The 1967 Detroit Riots From a Rooftop in Walled Lake," *Open Salon*, August 5, 2011. http://open.salon.com/blog /jeff_howe. Copyright © 2011 by Jeff L. Howe. All rights reserved. Reproduced by permission.

Last week [July 2011] marked the 44th anniversary of rioting in Detroit so severe that the effects there are still being felt. This is an account from the rural suburbs.

A "City Problem"

The night sky to the southeast glowed a smoldering orange the color of embers, and from the roof of a neighbor's house, the glow bounced off low clouds causing the reflection of flames to dance like the Northern Lights. The night air was thick and stagnant and smelled like a garbage fire suddenly doused with water. It was the summer of '67 and Detroit was burning.

And we were over forty miles away.

It had started in the wee hours of a Sunday morning, outside a bar in the black section of Detroit. It spread rapidly, both on the street and in the news. But for the first 48 hours it remained a stubborn but distant "city problem." It had nothing to do with us. It was simply a disturbing set of images in the newspaper and on the evening news.

> We were shocked as we watched on TV: row after row, block after block of homes being destroyed.

But by the third night it began to escalate to new levels of destruction. We were shocked as we watched on TV: row after row, block after block of homes being destroyed. It didn't make sense—black people seemed to be killing and destroying their own. The police forces were being overrun, the National Guard was called in, the President became involved. There seemed to be no end to it. In the suburbs, white families were becoming uneasy.

Coming for Walled Lake

At the height of the rioting, on the third or fourth night, I was hanging out at a little local miniature golf course/pizza joint with some friends when a car came tearing into the gravel parking lot with lights flashing and horn blaring. The owner of the car pulled to a stop and ran into the snack shop screaming something terrifying and unintelligible. Moments later the owner's voice came over the loudspeaker informing us that "the n-----s are burning their way out Northwestern Highway and are heading for Walled Lake!" The golf course was closing, he ordered, and he shut down the lights.

> Fathers were shouldering the family shotguns and climbing to the rooftops to defend their homes and their families.

What followed was one of the strangest nights I've ever experienced. Word spread like wildfire—by phone and word of mouth—and by the time I got home, fathers were shouldering the family shotguns and climbing to the rooftops to defend their homes and their families from the hordes of savages advancing from the city like an army of ants.

Battle plans were devised, ammo was gathered from gun lockers and closet shelves, units were deployed in station wagons and pickup trucks, and daughters were locked in basements. All night long I laid awake in bed to the sounds of angry, frightened voices, squealing tires and occasional gunshots from outside my window. And when morning came, it revealed a small battalion of fathers and older brothers on the rooftops of our neighborhood, lying in wait for whatever came next.

Well, of course, nothing came next. Although the riots lasted for five days and caused the destruction of entire sections of downtown Detroit, it never came even remotely close to Walled Lake. It turns out that what DID happen was that someone robbed a hardware store out on Haggarty Road, hoping to go unnoticed in the melee. A single, isolated robbery fifteen miles away caused a rumor that had spread faster than a shock wave out through the obviously nervous and terrified suburbs.

It was anger, fear and misinformation that created the environment for the riots to begin in the first place. It was anger, fear and misinformation that caused them to spread. And it was anger, fear and misinformation that fanned them through the suburbs like a wildfire traveling at the speed of a rumor.

And it produced a night exactly like the one that many of the fathers in our neighborhood—mostly World War II veterans—had been preparing for all their lives. Damn the ideals, families were at stake. At least that's what it seemed like to a sixteen-year-old. That's how thick the night air was during that week in the summer of '67 when Detroit was burning.

An Educator Recalls the 1967 Detroit Riots in the Summer After Her High School Graduation

Doreen Cato

In the following viewpoint, a children's rights advocate remembers the Detroit riots, which occurred the summer after she graduated from high school. The author discusses the discrimination and disillusionment that led to the riots. She also describes seeing fires and explosions and the National Guard enter the city. She says that the experience was traumatic, and she still has nightmares about the riots. Doreen Cato is the executive director at First Place, a school and social service agency for homeless and vulnerable children and families in Seattle, Washington.

SOURCE. Doreen Cato, "Chapter 7: A Community at War," *Saving the Leader Within: The Impact of Childhood Trauma on Leadership*. AuthorHouse, 2011, pp. 75–85. Copyright © 2011 by Doreen Cato. All rights reserved. Reproduced by permission.

It was June of 1967 and I had graduated from high school. It should have been a happy day, but for some odd reason my father appeared to be in a strange mood. After graduation exercises we went straight home. I do not know what I was expecting, but I thought a small gift or family party was well warranted. I had not only graduated on time, but many of my acquaintances who lived in the community were either pregnant, had dropped out of school, or were behind academically while I was on my way to college. Only a few of us had been accepted into a university. It was a day to rejoice! So why did my father appear to be angry at me? I found out many years later.

Causes of the Riots

At one point during his final two years of life, I read portions of this work to my father, including my description of my high-school graduation. With tears in his eyes he had this to say about that day, "I came to realize that my oldest child was no longer my baby and would be eventually going to college and I was not emotionally or mentally ready to lose you yet." In this moment I noticed myself letting go of the old rage I still harbored toward him. Simultaneously, I noticed the tension in my neck and stomach subsiding. I realized it was time to learn to accept him unconditionally and hope he would someday do the same with me.

I spent most of the summer trying to get hired to raise money for college. This was a difficult task because I was short, small in stature, and looked underage. One of my father's older sisters, who lived in Ann Arbor, managed to get me a job at St. Joseph Mercy Hospital, as a nurse's aide. She also generously made room for me to live with her at her home during my first two years at school. I was scheduled to start my new job during the first week of August. Four days before I was supposed to leave for my new job in Ann Arbor, thirty miles away, the city of Detroit erupted in a riot. It is important to provide a little background to illustrate what lead to such devastation and the current consequences of upheaval in Detroit's infrastructure, with its limited growth economy, lack of employment and one third of all inner city homes condemned.

By 1967, disillusionment had replaced exhilaration and many proponents of social justice had lost motivation to fight for civil rights. Following Dr. King Jr.'s march in 1963, the earlier elation began to erode and [the] community's anger was slowly turning into rage. Why? Due to corrupt lending practices and misguided urban renewal, many of Detroit's Black residents lacked adequate housing. Detroit had held the highest homeownership rate among Black people in the nation, but during this period urban renewal projects bulldozed some Black neighborhoods to make way for freeway construction. In order to construct Interstate 75, entire neighborhoods were demolished, displacing most residents into high-rise low-income project housing or already-crowded neighborhoods. The focus of the Black communities' concern was the loss of an area called Black Bottom. This was a popular, much loved Detroit neighborhood where many Blacks would gather to socialize at restaurants, nightclubs and theaters and worship at churches. The destruction of this neighborhood resulted in racial tensions due to the loss of community as well as the loss of housing.

> Blacks were denied the ability to move to many neighborhoods, including most of the Detroit suburbs.

Additionally, corrupt lending practices by financial institutions, such as red-lining [in which lenders refused to lend to blacks], restricted the areas where Blacks could live and own property. This meant that in addition to deed restrictions in local communities, Blacks were denied the ability to move to many neighborhoods, including most of the Detroit suburbs. Many homes that were privately owned were bought on land contract at high interest rates and with very short foreclosure schedules. Blacks were trapped and confined to often undesirable areas that were insufficient to hold the displaced population. According to [John] Hersey's (1967) article in *Time* magazine, by 1967 the neighborhood around 12th Street had a population density that was twice the city average. Black schools in the city were overcrowded and underfunded. In the 1960s, Detroit's total population was shrinking due to White flight although the Black population continued to rapidly increase, due to continued migration from the South. By 1966 Detroit was losing over 20,000 residents a year, most of them White. They left for new jobs, better housing, better city services and better schools in the suburbs. Partially in response to Detroit taxes, Detroit lost 134,000 jobs from 1947 to 1963. Between 1946 and 1956, General Motors spent $3.4 billion on new plants, Ford $2.5 billion, and Chrysler $700 million, opening a total of 25 auto plants, all in Detroit's suburbs. Meanwhile, between 1950 and 1970, Detroit's inner city lost around 240,000 residents. By 1967 the city government was in deep financial trouble as the property tax base dropped. Whites could escape the problems of Detroit, but Blacks were denied loans and, in many cases, the chance to purchase homes in the suburbs.

In 1967, the Detroit Police Department was predominantly White and only 5% Black. Among the Black residents of Detroit the Department's Big Four or Tactical Squads, each made up of four police officers, had a reputation for harassment and brutality. Officers verbally degraded youths, and those that could not produce proper identification were often arrested or worse. My twelve year old brother was one of those individuals. Several questionable shootings and beatings of Blacks by officers were reported by the local press in the years preceding 1967. After the riot, a *Detroit Free Press* survey

Detroit police officers confront pedestrians during the July 1967 riots. The negative relationship between the police and African American residents contributed greatly to the tragedy. (© Lee Balterman/Time & Life Pictures/Getty Images.)

cited in the *Time* magazine article "12th Street Riot" revealed that Detroit residents reported police brutality as the number one problem they faced in the period leading up to the riot. My eyewitness account of what happened in July 1967 during what was to become known as the infamous Detroit riot [follows].

An Eyewitness Account

It began as a hot muggy evening and I went to say good-bye to a dear friend before leaving for Eastern Michigan University. I had promised to come and spend the night with her before I left for Ann Arbor. Our parents were out of town together and my siblings were at home happy that I was gone as well. We were sitting on her front porch when we heard what we thought were firecrackers going off near Twelfth Street. *The skin on the back of my neck suddenly feels clammy just as it did on that hot humid evening.* My father's oldest sister lived on the corner of Euclid and Twelfth, near Claremont where the afterhours bar, the Blind Pig, was located. Detroit police raided the bar that night, and sparked the riot. It would be three days before I saw my sisters and brother again.

My friend and I were caught in the middle of all this chaos. We woke up at eight o'clock the following morning to hear people driving down the street laughing and screaming. I looked out the window and saw three men carrying bottles with rags sticking out of them running towards Lynnwood Avenue. I remember laughing with surprise because the sight seemed so bizarre. The world had gone crazy that day.

> The fire trucks were trying to get through, but people were throwing stones.

Suddenly, two blocks over, the local gas station blew up, taking out the five surrounding brick homes. We rushed to put on our clothes to go help any survivors. Luckily, many people had gone to work already. Once we were outside I looked down the street to where my father's oldest sister lived and saw a wall of fire. Twelfth Street was entirely up in flames and the paint store on Lynnwood Street was also on fire. The fire trucks were trying to get through, but people were throwing stones. Finally, one man came out of his house with a rifle and shot it into the air saying if another person threw a stone he was going to shoot them. I remember thinking, "My God! What is going on? Are we at war?" As my friend and I looked at the corner gas station near her home, there was an explosion at the paint store on the opposite corner that knocked us to the ground. This is when we came to the realization we were really in danger because the gas station two houses away from her home was also on fire. The man next door started watering down his roof. There was so much smoke, fire, and mayhem that at first we did not know what to do. We ran to help the people where the first gas station had blown up. We kept asking each other, "Where are the police?" We were surrounded by flames and fear.

The National Guard Enters the City

In the meantime, unbeknownst to us, my father and her mother were trying to get back into Detroit. The bridge that led to my family home had been raised to prevent any looters from getting near Dearborn or other predominantly White areas. It was comforting to know my siblings were away from most of the horror. As for the question about the whereabouts of the police, rumor had it they were protecting the White neighborhoods. Watching a troop of armed, all-White National Guardsmen marching down our neighborhood streets was the scariest sight. There has been some speculation that the deployment of troops incited more violence during the riot. It is true that National Guard troops were engaged in firefights with locals. These fights resulted in deaths both to locals and the troops. Tanks and machine guns were used in the effort to keep the peace. Film footage and photos shown internationally were of a city on fire, with tanks and combat troops in firefights in the streets, sealing Detroit's reputation for decades to come. This was not mentioned in any of the local papers. They invaded our community with their fear. Did they truly intend to maintain peace or just forcefully demand order? I only know this invasion brought more violence and destruction to my world. Because of this experience I can truly empathize with people whose countries have been invaded.

Although I did not know it, by that evening, I was in shock. I was sitting on my friend's porch trying to make sense of this new world when I realized I had not eaten anything all day. The electricity, phone and water were out, but I thought there might be some food at the corner store that appeared to still be operating. Due to my condition of shock, I was unaware of the Guardsman at the bottom of the walkway and also of the fact that we were temporarily living under Martial Law[1] with an enforced curfew. As I was walking towards the corner store a young guardsman pointed his rifle at me and ordered me to stop. I did not think he was speaking to me because I was unarmed. There was sniper fire going on and off in the distance throughout the evening which seemed unreal. I remember asking myself in a dreamlike state, "How could there be sniper fire here, this is the city for goodness sake?" Nevertheless, for the first time in my life I had a gun in my face and it was in the hands of a frightened White boy. If I had taken one more step I believe he would have shot me. I went back and sat on the porch step visibly shaken looking out at the destruction. *To this day the smell of stale smoke will sometimes bring back the screaming in my head from that time.*

> If I had taken one more step I believe [a Guardsman] would have shot me.

I remember sitting there watching a Black man down at the corner. He was sitting on the sidewalk crying and talking about losing his cat in a house fire. His home was one of those that went up in flames earlier, after the first gas station exploded. The man who had shot his rifle into the air earlier in the day had scared the looters away from the gas station next to us, and the firemen were able to put out the fire and save my friend's home. That was the last time we saw any firefighters after the crew saved my friend's and neighbors' homes. Apparently, they were asked to decline any incoming calls for help because it was considered too dangerous to enter our neighborhoods. This also explains why there was so much smoke and so many fires burning unchecked. My friend had to make me get up from the porch to find safety.

Later, during the night, a sniper managed to get up on her roof. We heard a Guardsman say "Shoot out that light," referring to the street light next to her house. My father, who managed to get through the barricade the morning of the second day, shared his memories of that day.

Snipers Emerge

As I was looking down from the window that evening a White state trooper was telling one of the seven troopers below to shoot out the light to stop the snipers from seeing them. I believe the snipers were Vietnam vets, because of the way the battle was fought throughout the night. There was no way ordinary citizens could fight with that kind of precision and using those tactical maneuvers. You had to have been in the service to fight the way they did. It was guerilla warfare.

The Guardsman and state troopers could not find the snipers. This, I believe, caused the governor to call for the army to come and stop the riot. I tried to make sense of what was happening. The National Guardsmen had fired at the light and missed twice. Finally the sniper said "I'll get it" and shot out the light. Quickly following this, the National Guard began shooting at the house. We were inside screaming, "We are inside! Stop for God's sake, we are inside!" *As I tell this part of the story I am sobbing out loud, because I realize now just how close we came to becoming casualties of war. I must stop and take a pause.*

Once the National Guardsmen began shooting, we heard the sniper run across the roof. We figured he knew the neighborhood, because the Guardsmen were unable to catch him. Only someone who knew my friend's neighborhood would know about the short cuts through the alleys. Later that night the Guardsmen repeated their actions and shot into another home, only this time they killed a four year old child. *I find I have to stop and pause again because of how difficult it is to bring back these old memories or should I say the horrors of the past.*

At this point the war was only beginning since the Guardsmen were having trouble keeping both Black and White looters out of the stores. By the second day, when it looked like the riots were getting closer to the White neighborhoods, the army was called in to help. Now this was a day to remember, tanks rolling down our city streets to be used against us and they did use them that day on several apartment buildings. The army received some misinformation that a particular apartment building was harboring snipers. People were running away and screaming a warning that the army was planning to shoot into an apartment building near Twelfth Street. I thought they were mistaken because this was not Vietnam, and then I heard the loud boom. I guess I was wrong. After this horrendous event, tensions ran high between the White army and the Black community causing smaller riots, protests, and sit-ins. The new generation was rebelling and held very strong beliefs. Many times these beliefs led to violence.

> "When it looked like the riots were getting closer to the White neighborhoods, the army was called in to help."

A White Person's Perspective

It is important to read a White person's perspective of the riot. This perspective provides a clear picture of how divided the Blacks and Whites were at that time. This account was written by a White woman who felt compelled to comment on the riot, yet was not in the rioting area. This is a known fact, because Detroit was under Martial Law and all White people were asked not to enter the affected areas. This account was retrieved from the internet in 2004. It is taken from a newspaper article featuring a description of the riot given by a woman named Sophie who resided outside the inner city of Detroit:

One of the worst riots in United States history was in Detroit, Michigan. On July 23, 1967, police raided an illegal bar in the city. They arrested some people. Before the police left a crowd had gathered outside the bar. This led to protest. The same night that small protest turned into mobs of people looting buildings, burning, and committing random acts of violence. Thousands of people were out in the streets. Hundreds of properties were damaged. Some believe this happened because of a lack of police intervention. But the police at the time said they did not want to send in police. In past riots police were sent in early and this sparked more violence and destruction. So the Detroit city police held back on sending in police. The rioting continued through the night. By morning it had gotten out of control. Police were helpless against the mobs of people protesting, burning and looting. There were fights in the streets, and many people were injured or arrested. The civil disturbance turned into a race riot. Different racial groups were fighting Whites and only burnt Black businesses or homes and same for Blacks. On the second night of the riot Blacks came from other parts of the city to help fight with other Blacks. The city was divided into sections of Black and White. The section that was a mixture was stuck between the two, where some people joined in the riot with people of the same race. Others would not join, which many times led to their house or business being burned. They were also subject to physical violence. All the hate from the past that people thought was gone came back out into the open. Blacks were at a lower standard. Racism raged through the streets. On the third day army troops were brought into the city. This was the first time anything other than police had to be used in a riot. The troops and police used tear gas and night sticks. Dogs were brought in to keep people controlled, but nothing would stop the people who felt strongly about getting rid of the other group. The police combined with army troops, finally gained control of the thousands of people raging through the city. When the riot was over fourteen square miles of urban neighborhoods had been destroyed. Forty-three people had been killed, seven thousand arrested, one thousand three hundred buildings destroyed, and two thousand seven hundred businesses looted. The riot was heard on radios and TVs across the country.

This newspaper account of the event fails to mention the National Guard being sent into our neighborhoods a full day before the army. To this day when I smell the scent of stale smoke it is accompanied by the memory of death and destruction followed by the sound of screaming in my head. When this happens I must find a calm place to quiet the screaming. In therapy, I later came to realize that these are my own screams I am hearing in my head. I returned home from the war, wearing a once bright yellow shell that was now black and feeling totally exhausted from three days of living in constant fear and terror. I will never forget those three horrific days. I still have an occasional nightmare about the riot or smell smoke where there is none. I am sure there are many of us who were at the epicenter of the riot who are still experiencing episodes of post-traumatic stress disorder from those unforgettable days. What many forget is that this was the second damaging race riot in Detroit's history. The first occurred in 1943, was also instigated by Whites and left over forty people dead.

Remarkably, on the fourth day, I left for my new job in Ann Arbor, one day later than planned. *I still wonder*

> " I still have an occasional nightmare about the riot or smell smoke where there is none. "

how it was possible that the horrors of three days appeared not to touch me at the time. The nursing staff was surprised to see me. They thought no one could get in or out of Detroit. However, I had been determined to leave after I made sure my sisters and brother were safe. Yet, I also wondered how I was able to bounce back from such a horrific experience as though nothing happened. This behavior proved to be a consistent pattern of how I would deal with other traumatic incidents in the future. I had apparently learned how to unconsciously remove myself from the situation in order to function according to societal norms.

Note

1. The author is speaking figuratively; martial law—the imposition of military rule over a civilian area as an emergency security measure—was not used during the riots.

The Big Bang

Coleman Young and Lonnie Wheeler

In the following viewpoint, a Michigan state senator remembers his experience during the Detroit riots. The author says that the events in Detroit were a rebellion and argues that they were not racially motivated. He contends that the racism of the police force was responsible for the violence escalating out of control. He describes his efforts to bring law enforcement officials to justice for their role in brutalizing civilians in the Algiers Motel incident. He also argues that Detroit mayor Jerome Cavanagh's refusal to bring the police to account alienated the black community and resulted in his political defeat. Coleman Young was a Detroit politician and the first African American mayor of the city, serving from 1974 to 1993.

The newsmagazines called Detroit a model city. They marveled at its strong chin and gushed over the heroic benevolence of Mayor Cavanagh, who had become the gallant knight of the War on Poverty by spearing forty-two million federal dollars for the city's poor people. Cavanagh was widely portrayed as a sort of

SOURCE. Excerpted from *Hard Stuff: The Autobiography of Coleman Young*, by Coleman Young and Lonnie Wheeler. New York: Viking, 1994. Used by permission of the Author's Estate.

Great White Sympathizer, and the fact is, he worked hard at maintaining a symbiotic rapport with black leaders. In that spirit, he had established an amicable relationship that led observers to think of Detroit as being immunized against the outbreak of inner-city rioting that had torn apart Watts in 1965, bloodied Chicago and Philadelphia, and in 1967 was sweeping the country at a rate that would produce 164 incidents, among them, major revolts in Cleveland and Newark.

Despite the mainstream feeling that it couldn't happen in Detroit (a sentiment that was not unanimously observed in the black community, where it was common knowledge that the mayor's goodwill had failed to impress his police officers), Cavanagh had taken the extra step of setting up an Early Warning Commission to alert him at the first hint of a disturbance. The only problem was that an urban riot is generally not an independent organism, welling up by its own exclusive devices, but entails an implicit partnership with an outside party. This is where the police come in.

What they did in the dark early morning of July 23, 1967, was raid a blind pig at 9125 Twelfth Street, near Clairmont, an inauspicious building with For Sale signs all around and "Economy Printing" painted on the front. The second floor was an informal meeting place called the Community League for Civil Action, where, at 3:45 A.M. that sweltering Sunday, scores of neighborhood folks were enjoying themselves in honor of servicemen home from Vietnam. The celebration ended when the police entered uninvited, threw somebody down the stairs, beat up a few others, and arrested more than eighty people.

The number of arrests proved to be most inopportune, because it required that many in the crowd be detained while the paddy wagon and squad cars ferried their friends to the precinct station. As that protracted process was taking place, others in the neighborhood began to close in on the scene until a swarm of hundreds had gathered. They taunted the police for their bullyish presence, and when somebody smashed the window of a squad car with a bottle, the bell went off on what the *Washington Post* called "the greatest tragedy of all [in] the long succession of Negro ghetto outbursts." By the time the glass hit the street, the crowd had become a mob, spilling garbage and setting it on fire, heaving bricks through store windows, and enthusiastically appropriating the merchandise therein.

Although the next few days are historically referred to as the Detroit riot, those in the black community still refer to it as a rebellion. I choose to think of it as an explosion—a chemical reaction to the prevailing conditions. The flammable element was police brutality, and when yet another measure of it was dropped into the beaker on July 23, the city went bang. As it was, the police might have neutralized the effects of the first fizz by mixing in peaceably, but they elected to agitate. Knowing that Cavanagh would disapprove of a full-scale action to quash the uprising, the cops brought in extra cruisers and menacingly circled the area, virtually inviting the defiance of the looters.

I was home from Lansing at the time, and many hours before I would have gotten up—remember, it was Sunday—I received a phone call from Louise Tappes, the wife of labor leader Shelton Tappes and a prominent community figure in her own right. The Tappeses lived in the vicinity of the blind pig that was raided, and from their back porch they witnessed the genesis of what was—prior to the Los Angeles rebellion of 1992—the most devastating week of urban violence in American annals. The first of sixteen hundred fires was set in a shoe store around 6:30 A.M. Later that morning, driving through the streets of west-central Detroit, I helplessly watched buildings go up in flames on Linwood and then on Dexter.

Just after noon, I was to attend a meeting with the mayor and other local leaders at Grace Episcopal Church on Twelfth Street, near the nucleus of the explosion. People were milling through the neighborhood in droves, and when I turned off West Grand Boulevard onto Twelfth, I came upon a crowd so thick it covered the streets and enveloped the church. Police lines prevented me from making it there. In fact, the meeting never came off, because none of the principals could get through. So I drove on and saw the destruction spread east to streets like Oakland and Clay.

> It became graphically evident that the black citizens were hell-bent on destroying the artifacts of their own haunted fate.

As the city was pillaged and burned, it became graphically evident that the black citizens were hell-bent on destroying the artifacts of their own haunted fate. John Conyers, a newly elected congressman and the son of a former patron of Maben's barbershop, climbed up on a car to address the mob through a bullhorn, and they stoned him down. When Reverend Nicholas Hood, the city's only black councilman, tried to calm his constituents, they threatened his life. The insurgents were going to do with their neighborhood what they would, and to hell with anybody who got in the way. The city hastily assembled an all-black firefighting unit to work the riot area, but it was pelted with debris and run off the scene.

As I made the rounds that day, 1 looked down the barrels of two or three police guns. Finally, I decided it was prudent to retreat home and monitor the goings-on from the front lawn of my apartment on East Forest, about a mile southeast of the heaviest action. But when I pulled into the neighborhood, I discovered that a liquor store had been burned down a few hundred feet from my place, across a vacant lot, and the apartment building had been evacuated because the wind was blowing the fire that way. Firemen hosed down the wall of the building as a precaution, and when the flames subsided, I pulled up a lawn chair and became a nervous spectator. From where I sat, the most unsettling sight wasn't the fire down the street but the caravans of police cars that rolled by with shotguns sticking out of the cruiser windows and station wagon tailgates. A couple of the officers ordered me inside the building, despite its condition, and although my custom would be to press the point, I also made it a rule not to argue with live ammunition in the heat of a major riot.

Remarkably, nobody was killed the first day. In that regard, the contrast with the 1943 riot was distinct, the earlier one having started and ended with white and black people murdering each other. The explosion of 1967, unlike the one twenty-four years before, was not a race riot. To be sure, most of the participants were black, and there were unmistakable racial implications, as suggested by the words "Soul Brother" and "Afro All the Way" painted on store windows by merchants who hoped that their businesses would be passed over by the looters. That strategy might have bought the owners an extra day or so, but it failed to spare them indefinitely, because the uprising was not a color dispute. A television cameraman took pictures of the looting of an A&P store on Trumbull, and there was racial unity up and down the goddamn aisles of that place. Blacks and whites were helping each other carry out cases of canned goods in complete harmony. Later, a survey was taken of those arrested during the week, the vast majority of who were black, and in answer to a question about whether their actions were antiwhite in nature, ninety-one percent said no.

It could be argued that the rebellion—specifically, the pillaging part of it—was as much about consumerism as about race, a revolt of underprivileged, over-crowded, hot, and irritable citizens who were fed up with having their meager economic means exploited by the privileged and finally had a chance to be the takers. I'd be surprised if there was a television left in any store in the inner city when the week was over. In fact, TV was a vital two-way player in the brutal game being carried out in the streets. For a week, people had been watching and getting ideas from TV coverage of the riot in Newark. They'd seen clips of similar events in Memphis and Milwaukee and Boston and Tampa and Cincinnati and Buffalo earlier in the summer. In that sense, TV represented the riot textbook. And on the other end, a television was the consummate looting item—an expensive, useful thing that could be carted off conspicuously. One of the most ironic and revealing snapshots of the week came when a looter was asked by a reporter how he liked the television he stole, and replied, "Not so good. The first thing I saw on it was me stealing the damn thing."

The looting was a cooperative effort in more than the racial context. Some observers testified that it was also government-assisted in a fashion, reporting National Guardsmen among those making off with merchandise. The Guard's ultimate role in the explosion, discharged with jitters, inexperience, and common bigotry, was to keep the fuel coming. Between the Guard and the police, authorities did their damnedest to turn the affair into a race riot, the operative word on their part being "n----r." Witnesses and photographs implicated police and Guardsmen in a horrific litany of offenses, among them: stabbing their arrest victims—many of them bystanders—with bayonets; fondling women's breasts; burning initials into a prisoner's back with a cigarette; and fire-bombing an Afro-American bookstore. The police attitude was aptly illustrated by an incident in which a black officer, Ike McKinnon, was driving home after a tense twenty-four-hour shift on the first day of the explosion. A white cop in a cruiser pulled him over for no discernible reason, and when the patrolman approached, McKinnon said, "Hi, police officer here." The other officer responded by shouting, "Get your black ass out of the car." When McKinnon showed his badge, the cop shot at him, fortunately missing.

> If the insurrection of Detroit in 1967 must be called a riot, let it be recorded as a police riot.

If the insurrection of Detroit in 1967 must be called a riot, let it be recorded as a police riot. This is not to say that the citizens of Detroit were justified in destroying their own community, or that the police should bear all of the blame; only that there was a principal object of the rebels' vengeance, and it was not the generic white man (though he was on the list), and it was not the white man behind the counter (though he was high on the list); it was the white man in the blue uniform.

When they understood the mess they were in, the police set up a riot command post at Herman Kiefer Hospital, between Twelfth and the Lodge Freeway. I can't tell you what went on there. In fact, the government's strategic process as a whole was something of a riddle—particularly the deliberations of Governor Romney, whose indecision and political machinations resulted in deadly delays. Romney was quick enough to declare a state of emergency and to order in state police and National Guardsmen, but it was immediately obvious that they only quickened the prevailing anxieties. The situation clearly called for federal troops (an assessment that places me in the uncomfortable role of agreeing with Walter Reuther, who appealed to the governor to place the order), but for some reason which defies any explanation save that of political posturing, Romney was reluctant to request them. It was well-known that Romney was positioning himself for a run at the presidency in 1968, and if he were to succeed in winning the Republican nomination, which was not an outlandish prospect, he would presumably find himself pitted against President Johnson. As a candidate, he shrank at the prospect of appealing to his opponent to bail him out of an ugly problem in his own territory. In turn, Johnson was not above manipulating the situation to his political advantage.

By Sunday night, the inner city had become an open wound and the raw spot was spreading west to Grand River and Livernois and east to Mack Avenue while the governor f---ed around with protocol and face-saving language. At three A.M. Monday—nearly twenty-four hours after the first salvo—Romney mustered a call to Attorney General Ramsey Clark, asking for federal assistance. But he was still limp on the details, and it was eleven o'clock before Johnson sent in 4,700 paratroopers. Even then, the political pussy-footing had only just begun. Instead of sweeping straight into the raging city, the soldiers put down at Selfridge Air Base, forty miles from downtown. Late Monday evening, after the second and worst day of rioting, help moved a little closer when three units from the 101st and 82nd Airborne arrived at the state fairgrounds on the northern extremity of Detroit, Woodward and Eight Mile. At midnight, the President went on national television to explain the federal state of emergency that had necessitated military action, making numerous references in the course of his address to Romney's inability to handle the crisis with state and local resources. Finally, at three A.M. Tuesday—two full days after the riot had started and twenty-four hours after Romney had summoned the wherewithal to ask for troops—Airborne personnel in full battle dress checked into Southeastern High School to defend the east side of the city, which they proceeded to do skillfully.

The pre-established police concentration on the west side, near the center of the explosion, dictated that the paratroopers be deployed on the opposite part of town, which proved to be an uneven and unfortunate arrangement. On the west side, the community was virtually under siege. The state police and the National Guard were lily-white at the time, or damn near; and combined with the racist Detroit police, the effect was like a white army of occupation on both sides of Twelfth Street. The jackboots of the authorities were on the necks of the black community, and the community was squirming violently to get free. The parameters were confrontational, fostering a winless situation in which peace would represent surrender. It was no coincidence that most of the violence occurred in that vicinity. By contrast, the paratrooper outfits were thoroughly integrated, right up through the officers—quite a change from my Air Force days—and they were able to bring the east side under control swiftly and firmly with a light touch. They made it clear, with little more than professionalism and an attitude, that they were in place to protect the citizens, not to punish them. After two or three days, there was an air of fraternization on the east side completely unfamiliar in the oppressive police climate of Detroit.

> "The state police and the National Guard were lily-white at the time, . . . the effect was like a white army of occupation."

But the federal troops had arrived much too late to do anything about a tragic Monday, when an awful outbreak of fires accounted for more than six hundred alarms and the riot took its first victim, a white man who was shot while running from a store that had just been looted on Fourth Street. There would be forty-three people killed in all, thirty of them by law enforcement officials, and more than seven thousand three hundred arrested. In excess of four hundred buildings were destroyed, including twenty percent of the ones on Twelfth Street around Virginia Park. The riot hardly let up the whole damn week. Looting and sniping continued until Friday, and their side effect, price gouging—some of the stores that survived took advantage of the situation by charging up to four times the normal rates—was so rampant that the city council was required to pass an emergency ordinance to control it. Meanwhile, prisoners filled the state and federal penitentiaries, the county jail, the police gym and garages, and the bathhouse at Belle Isle, which looked like a goddamn war camp.

As the city quieted down, I became concerned that the police department might be overstepping its bounds in the effort to apprehend and punish those involved in the uprising. My fear was that we would see a repeat of what had occurred in Newark, where the police department had obtained a list of registered guns in the city, broken it down by precinct, and stormed through the neighborhoods kicking down doors and seizing legal weapons. Such an authoritarian tactic was a flagrant violation of civil rights and a frightening sign of oppression. To my knowledge, there was no comparable list circulating in the Detroit Police Department, but there were a disturbing number of reports about doors being kicked in. In reaction to those reports, John Conyers and I established a forum for citizens to air their complaints, setting up informal hearings at the Amalgamated Clothing Workers Hall, Twelfth Street and West Grand.

At one of the meetings, a young black man stood up and requested that we help his brother get out of jail to attend the funeral of another brother who had been killed in an incident at the Algiers Motel, a manor house on Woodward at Virginia Park renowned for its low-life activities. It was known that three people had been shot and killed at the Algiers during the rebellion, but the deaths had been reported as the result of violence initiated by guests at the motel.

When the young man began to tell an entirely different story, we realized that it was very hot stuff and advised him to say no more. We then interviewed him more privately at the Guardian Building law office of John's brother, Nathan Conyers, and followed up by bringing in additional witnesses. The result was a grisly, horrifying tale of wanton executions perpetrated by a combined force of city, state, and federal law-enforcement officers. Instrumental in reconstructing the events of the day were two white girls from Ohio, high school dropouts who had come to Detroit seeking adventure. They were very naive and soon found themselves in much faster company than they were prepared for. I don't think the girls were prostitutes, but no doubt some of the guys they were involved with were pimps who would have liked to turn them out. In the meantime, the girls were letting their hair down in the sort of activity that was common to the Algiers, and when the cops arrived in response to false reports of sniping at the motel, they apparently went nuts at the sight of white girls in the company of black men. According to the survivors, the lawmen busted in, rounded up everyone on the premises, and proceeded to brutalize the entire party with a twisted "death game" in which they ordered each person into a separate room, one by one, and fired shotguns to make the others believe—sometimes accurately, sometimes not—that he or she had been killed. In the process, three innocent people were shot dead for the hell of it.

When we fully comprehended the scope of what we were hearing, Conyers and I decided to call in the Justice Department. You can imagine how distasteful that was for me, given my history with the Justice motherf-----s; but it was either them or the police, and we sure as hell couldn't trust the police. The newspapers and the county prosecutor joined in the investigation, and the case against the officers made it to state court on charges of second-degree murder. It was a sensational, highly publicized trial, during which it was revealed that there had been no exchange of fire at the Algiers, and that the victims had been shot at a range so close that there were powder burns on their flesh and shotgun shells embedded in their wounds. Despite all of that, the jury, acting upon the judge's charge that the officers had to be found innocent unless it could be proven they had "killed with malice and premeditation," allowed the defendants to walk free. Nobody was ever convicted for what happened at the Algiers Motel. I issued a press release that said, "This latest phase of a step-by-step whitewash of a police slaying demonstrates once again that law and order is a one-way street. There is no law and order where black people are involved, especially when they are involved with the police."

> The Detroit Police Department . . . [was] ill equipped to maintain order or represent justice in the inner city.

It apparently took a rebellion and a major controversy for Cavanagh to recognize that the defining whiteness of the Detroit Police Department—in both numbers and mentality—left it ill equipped to maintain order or represent justice in the inner city. When he did, he established a committee to address the matter of affirmative action in the department. I was appointed to the committee, but soon found that I was butting up against the hard heads of the law enforcement establishment, which was loath to integrate the department in the equitable proportions advocated by me and the black citizenry. The police unions were politically powerful—they could make or break an elected city official—and Cavanagh yielded to their pressure, backing off from any substantial affirmative-action initiatives. He and I fell out over that. When Jerry sided with the police, I felt I had no alternative but to publicly resign my committee position in protest. Before the riot, many blacks had been willing to give Cavanagh the benefit of the doubt, presuming that he had no control over the actions of individual police officers; but when he had the perfect opportunity to change the complexion of the department by administering bold affirmative-action measures, he faltered conspicuously. With that, the black community began to perceive the mayor as an uncertain trumpet, and he lost a lot of constituents because of it. Ultimately, Cavanagh became another casualty of the rebellion.

An Author Recalls How the Riots Interrupted Her Wedding Party

Theresa Welsh

In the following viewpoint, a white Detroit resident describes the day of her wedding party, which occurred during the riots of 1967. She was living in a building occupied mostly by whites, and she discusses the fear, anxiety, and racism of some of her neighbors. The author maintains that the rioters were not trying to harm white people, but were instead angry at police and at the white power structure. She says that the riot caused permanent damage to the city. She details returning to the city years later and being shocked at houses, streets, and stores that had been abandoned. Theresa Welsh is an author and technical writer.

I grew up in Flint, Michigan, a classic company town. General Motors ruled, with factory smoke stacks dominating the cityscape and my family's home lo-

---

SOURCE. Theresa Welsh, "Detroit: From Industrial Giant to Empty Landscape," The Seeker Books. www.theseekerbooks.com. Copyright © by Theresa Welsh. All rights reserved. Reproduced by permission.

cated in the shadow of the Buick plant where my Dad worked. When I was just a little child, my sister and I used to run to meet my Dad as he walked home from work and fight over who got to carry his lunch pail. There was a nice park between where our street ended and the factory. My Dad worked for Buick for over 40 years before retiring with a pension and health care benefits (he died at age 92 in 2004). The auto industry was good for Flint, and no one would have thought that a day would come when they would NOT build Buicks in Flint, just like no one could imagine that General Motors would one day go bankrupt.

Moving to Detroit

I attended Catholic schools and graduated in 1962 from St Michael High School in Flint, and could hardly wait to leave this dreary factory town. While growing up, I had loved going to the Big City—Detroit—to see the Detroit Tigers play baseball. My Dad was a huge Tigers fan and so was I. I found the area around the stadium, with its big old houses, fascinating and always wanted to see more of the city. With a scholarship to Wayne State University [WSU], I was delighted to leave Flint behind and take up residence in the Big City. Wayne State was just south of the New Center area, so-called because it was like a second downtown, dominated by the huge, ornate General Motors Building and, across West Grand Boulevard from it, the fabulous art deco Fisher Building. These buildings just oozed class and success. General Motors had popular brands of cars with Chevrolet, Buick, Oldsmobile, Pontiac, and that symbol of material success, Cadillac.

While there was considerable prosperity during the 1960s, Detroit was not uniformly a place that reflected that prosperity. The city had pockets of poverty and some commercial streets were full of liquor stores, pawn shops, pool halls, wig shops, and various marginal businesses, some of which turned into "blind pigs" at night. A "blind pig" is also known as an "after-hours joint." In plain language, that is a place that sells liquor by the glass after the hours when bars have to close. Neighborhoods on the East Side around Kercheval St had plenty of crime, and on the West Side, you had 12th St and Linwood Ave. Detroit was a racially segregated city, with black neighborhoods (mostly the high-crime areas) and white neighborhoods.

At WSU, I met David Welsh at the school newspaper office, where he was a student photographer. In 1967, we got married. We both had apartments on campus, and went looking for a place to share. We answered an ad for a place that the ad said was in the New Center area. However, it turned out to be at the corner of West Chicago and Linwood, a mainly black area. This building was one of two white buildings on Chicago Blvd. It was right across the street from Sacred Heart Seminary, where young men studied to become Catholic priests. We assumed the ad had placed it "in the New Center area" because they wanted to attract white people. The apartment was nice, so we took it.

I had watched my family endlessly argue about arrangements and expenses when my sister Barbara got married, so I felt strongly that I wanted none of that. I told David we should just go downtown to City Hall and find a judge, and so we did. I called my mother and told her I was getting married on Saturday downtown and she and Dad could come if they wanted to. Some of our friends came too, and we found a very nice judge who seemed delighted to conduct the short ceremony. One of our friends whipped out his wallet and paid the judge, while another produced a bottle of champagne. The wedding cost us nothing, and I have never regretted doing it this way.

My Wedding Party Was a Riot

However, my aunts and uncles back in Flint took offense at being deprived of a drunken party (like they'd had for my sister's wedding) and I got feedback that we should invite the relatives to our new apartment to make up for the lack of invitations to a "real" wedding. I made plans to have a buffet spread and a large sheet cake set up in the apartment, and I sent our invitations to my Flint family. The day for this gathering was Sunday, July 23, 1967. If you look up that date in Detroit history, you will find it was the day the 1967 riot began. And, yes, the riot began less than a mile from our apartment on West Chicago.

We were not aware of anything as my aunts, uncles and cousins filed into our apartment, which was on the first floor, down a short hall from the small lobby. Most brought us gifts, and we talked and laughed and ate and finally people began leaving. A few had mentioned that there seemed to be some disturbance on nearby streets which they had seen as they drove to our place. Once the relatives were gone, we became aware of noise and strange goings-on outside. We turned on our TV and discovered there was a serious disturbance centered on 12th street that was spilling over into nearby streets and threatening to engulf the West Side. This was not far from where we were now standing in our apartment, listening to the TV and, more to the point, hearing the actual sounds of the riot outside. We began talking with other residents of the building who were now congregating in the hallways.

> If it was a race riot, wouldn't we be targeted?

They were very worried because they felt it was the black people who were rioting and we were a little island (two buildings) of white people on a long block of solid black apartment buildings. If it was a race riot, wouldn't we be targeted?

I looked at the remains of the buffet table and the pile of gifts on the floor. What would happen to us? Had my relatives made it safely to the expressway? As we talked further with other residents, some went down in the basement to see if there might be anything useful for barricading ourselves or hiding. Some of the residents were pretty racist and wanted to join the fight—against the rioters. The manager of this building was a raging racist who used to refer to blacks as "jigs." It seemed odd that he would be living in a building surrounded by black people when he seemed to dislike them so much.

We, on the other hand, had experienced no problems with our neighbors in the area, and had frequently patronized the gas station on the corner of Linwood and Chicago for repairs to the badly-worn tires on our old car. The owner was a very fine black man named Leon Moon who would cheerfully add another patch to one of our tires when we suffered a flat. At times, the neighborhood did feel a bit alien though. If I was downtown, I would always take the Dexter bus, which involved a longer walk when getting off the bus, back to the apartment rather than the Linwood bus because I knew I would be the only white person on the Linwood bus and that made me feel uncomfortable. It was not that I feared actual danger from these black Detroiters, but rather that I would be the object of curiosity. What was a white girl doing in this all-black neighborhood? Sometimes I wasn't sure and I didn't want to face the question. The Dexter bus went up into a predominantly Jewish neighborhood, so there were usually at least a few other white people on the bus besides me.

I had not felt any hostility from any of our nearby black neighbors, but certainly our apartment manager was not kindly disposed toward them and no doubt some of them knew it. I was used to segregated housing patterns from living on campus at WSU, where the white students lived on the west side of Woodward Avenue and the black students lived on the east side of Woodward. But here we were, facing a sea of black people who were rioting in the streets. Not a good situation on this fateful day in 1967 as we contemplated the growing disturbances outside.

Fires in Every Direction

Inside our building, someone suggested going up on the roof for a better look at the extent of the rioting. I liked this idea and joined a few other people and located a stairway to the roof. When we got up there, I looked around in shock and disbelief. In every direction, there were fires. The city was burning. Some of the fires were close, and it was clear this would present a very large challenge to the city Fire Department. I stood there in a daze, wondering if we would all burn up. I will never forget the sight of the city of Detroit on fire.

Our cars were parked in a lot right next to the building. One of the men on the roof posed the question: what should we do if the rioters start messing with our cars? David quickly told him, "let them mess with the cars." It was clear that there was little we could do if the rioters decided to target us. I thought about random things like the fact that some of David's pants were in the nearby "40 Minute Cleaners," a building we would later find was a charred ruin. I was sorry my relatives had spent money on gifts, which might be destroyed before the day was over if the fires reached us. I wondered if I'd be able to go to work on Monday or even be alive on Monday. As it turned out, it was days before I would go to work. No one went to work in Detroit during those first days of the riot when the city was engulfed in turmoil.

From our apartment, we could hear gunshot sounds from every direction, and the National Guard rolled down Chicago Blvd in tanks, which they parked at a school just around the block on Linwood. Our bedroom faced an alley, and I was too afraid to sleep in the bed for fear of being shot through the windows. We could see looted items in piles in the alley and hear the looters laughing. We could hear the loud bang-bang of gunshots coming from back there. We slept (or tried to sleep) on the living room floor, which was the furthest spot from a window. When we finally ventured out, we found no one paying us any attention. There were many businesses in the commercial buildings on Linwood Street, and we found the Middle Eastern family who owned the little grocery store on Linwood sitting inside, holding rifles and looking out the window, challenging anyone to break into their store. The sight of those big guns had apparently kept their store from being ransacked, which had been the fate of many of the commercial storefronts. Up and down Linwood, stores and apartment buildings had placed signs that read "Soul Brother." This was to indicate it was black-owned. Sometimes this seemed to work, but mostly the rioters didn't care. They were having too much fun looting every place they could.

We also found the seminary across the street had not been spared, but it had not been looted either. Someone has taken black paint and painted the face of the statue of Jesus that stood on the lawn. That statue has remained like that, with a black-faced Jesus, all these years, a continuing legacy of the riots. You can see it yourself if you use the Google "street-level" mapping (look for the corner of Chicago and Linwood). There were certainly racial overtones to this horrendous event, but from our vantage point, it was not a "race riot" since our black neighbors never did turn on us and no one messed with our cars. It did not appear that blacks wanted to hurt whites, but rather many wanted to vent frustrations and, once the riot was underway, get some loot. Their anger was directed mainly at the police and their own economic disenfranchisement. Black unemployment was high, and white people dominated city government and the police department. Black people called this the "white power structure."

The riot had begun in the early hours of Sunday as the police raided a blind pig on 12th street. The Detroit

> From our vantage point, it was not a 'race riot' since our black neighbors never did turn on us.

The face of a statue of Jesus was painted by protesters in July 1967. It remains on the lawn of the Sacred Heart Major Seminary in the west side of Detroit as a permanent reminder of the riots. (© **Lee Balterman/Time & Life Pictures/Getty Images.**)

police at that time were mainly white, and [members of] the black community were too often victims of unfair treatment and brutality by the police. On this fateful day, their anger just spilled out and they did not go quietly to the paddy wagons. The riot spread gradually until the late afternoon, when my relatives were all driving back home (they all got out safely); it had engulfed a large part of the West Side. It continued to spread throughout the city that day and the days that followed.

After the Riot

In so many ways, the city has never recovered from the 1967 riot. The main commercial thoroughfares—Woodward Avenue, Grand River Avenue and Gratiot Avenue—were burned and looted and the gaping, empty storefronts remained fixtures for many years. Eventually, some were rebuilt and some torn down and replaced with new buildings, but even more just became empty lots. New commercial residents were few. Detroit became a city without grocery stores, where abandoned stores turned into little storefront churches where itinerant preachers set up shop or became liquor stores where big sheets of Plexiglas separated clerk from customer. . . .

Now that I'm getting old and have finally retired from a five-day-a-week job, I've initiated a project to go back into the city and see places where I've lived and worked and see what's happened to the city. It's been a shocking discovery. The city has been losing its people and the landscape is becoming empty. Streets that had houses where people lived and loved are now just vacant lots and abandoned buildings, with roofs caved in and trash piled on broken porches. Sidewalks are disappearing as weeds poke through cracks and take over the pavement. Commercial buildings stand empty, with gaping storefronts filled with trash and debris and stairways up to nowhere. Where have all the people gone?

> Streets that had houses where people lived and loved are now just vacant lots and abandoned buildings.

Sadly, this is happening all over Detroit. We have taken a number of touring, picture-taking trips throughout the city and have found large tracts of empty land in all parts of the city. Our old apartment building on West Chicago is gone, replaced by an empty field. There are only a few of the former buildings remaining, and up and down 12th street, where the riot began, are abandoned storefronts and empty lots, some now used for urban farming. The East Side has been particularly hard hit, with all of its formerly commercial thoroughfares reduced to weed-filled lots. In some places, whole neighborhoods are gone, and sometimes the streets have been closed off with concrete slabs so cars cannot enter what used to be streets full of houses. The amount of just plain emptiness is shocking and hard to describe in words alone, or even to capture in pictures. This is abandonment. Most of the empty houses stand wide open. You can walk right in the front door and see piles of stuff: broken pieces of furniture, dishes, clothes, etc. Did someone just walk out and leave their life behind? How does this abandonment happen?

CHRONOLOGY

1943   June 20: Riots breaks out in Detroit as young blacks and whites fight with each other.

1950s   The white population of Detroit begins to leave the city as African Americans move in.

Early 1960s   The black neighborhoods of Paradise Valley and Black Bottom in Detroit are largely destroyed by urban renewal projects and freeway construction.

1962   Black prostitute Shirley Scott is shot in the back and killed by Detroit police.

1964   Barbara Jackson, a black prostitute, and Howard King, a black teenager, are beaten in separate incidents by Detroit police.

1967   June 26: Rioting begins in Buffalo, New York.

    July 1: Rioting in Buffalo ends.

    July 12: Rioting begins in Newark, New Jersey.

    July 17: Rioting in Newark ends.

    July 23: Police raid a club in Detroit where African Americans are celebrating the return of Vietnam veterans. The conflict escalates into a riot.

    July 24: The Michigan State Police is called in to help Detroit police. The violence escalates.

July 25: President Lyndon Johnson sends National Guard troops into Detroit. They are later joined by army paratroopers.

July 26: Policemen and National Guardsmen storm the Algiers Motel in the early morning hours. They kidnap and beat the people inside, killing three.

H. Rap Brown, an activist and advocate of black power, is arrested for inciting a riot in Maryland.

July 27: The National Guard and Army bring the riot in Detroit under control, though some critics claim their actions initially escalated the violence and resulted in unnecessary deaths.

President Johnson appoints the Kerner Commission to assess the causes of violence and rioting.

1968   February 29: The Kerner Commission report is released. It blames rioting on segregation, racism, and inequality.

1970   Detroit mayor Jerome Cavanagh declines to run for reelection and steps down. His political reputation is seriously damaged by the 1967 riots.

1974   Coleman Young becomes the first black mayor of Detroit.

FOR FURTHER READING

Books

Paul Clemens, *Made in Detroit*. New York: Anchor Books, 2005.

Bruce J. Dierenfield, *The Civil Rights Movement: Revised Edition*. Harlow, UK: Pearson, 2008.

Reynold Farley, *Detroit Divided*. New York: Russell Sage Foundation Publications, 2002.

Sidney Fine, *Violence in the Model City: The Cavanagh Administration, Race Relations, and the Detroit Riot of 1967*. East Lansing: Michigan State University Press, 2007.

Andra Gillespie, *Whose Black Politics?: Cases in Post-Racial Black Leadership*. New York: Routledge, 2010.

Peniel E. Joseph, ed., *The Black Power Movement: Rethinking the Civil Rights—Black Power Era*. New York: Routledge, 2006.

Kevin M. Kruse, *White Flight: Atlanta and the Making of Modern Conservatism*. Princeton, NJ: Princeton University Press, 2005.

Lindsey Lupo, *Flak Catchers: One Hundred Years of Riot Commission Politics in America*. Lanham, MD: Lexington Books, 2011.

Scott Martell, *Detroit: A Biography*. Chicago, IL: Chicago Review Press, 2012.

Thomas J. Sugrue, *The Origins of the Urban Crisis: Race and Inequality in Postwar Detroit, Revised Edition*. Princeton, NJ: Princeton University Press, 2005.

Periodicals

Barry Barkan, "2 Policemen Charged in Riot Deaths," *Washington Post*, August 8, 1967.

Louis Cook, "Struggling Detroit: Head Up, Chin Out 10 Years After Riot," *Washington Post*, July 31, 1977.

Darrell Dawsey, "Been a Long Time Coming," *The Detroit Blogs—Time*, September 24, 2009. www.time.com.

Peter Dreier, "Riot and Reunion: Forty Years Later," *Nation*, July 17, 2007. www.thenation.com.

Edgar Z. Friedenberg, "Motown Justice," *New York Review of Books*, August 1, 1968.

GlobalSecurity.org, "Detroit Riot of 1967," May 7, 2011.

Charles M. Hagen, "Algiers Motel," *Harvard Crimson*, July 12, 1968. www.thecrimson.com.

Celeste Headlee, "Riots Rocked Detroit 40 Years Ago Today," NPR, July 23, 2007. www.npr.org.

Michael Hirsley, "Detroit," *Chicago Tribune*, May 22, 1977.

Alex Klein and Matthew Zeitlin, "Chaos on the Streets of London, and History's Other Worst Riots," *New Republic*, August 10, 2011. www.tnr.com.

Rich Lowry, "The City That Liberalism Ruined," *National Review*, April 1, 2008. www.nationalreview.com.

Bill McGraw, "The Rise and Fall of Kwame Kilpatrick," *Detroit News*, September 5, 2008. www.freep.com.

Robyn Meredith, "5 Days in 1967 Still Shake Detroit," *New York Times*, July 23, 1997. www.nytimes.com.

John J. Miller, "A City on Fire," *National Review*, July 30, 2002. http://old.nationalreview.com.

New York Times, "Editorial: The Responsibility: White and Black," July 30, 1967.

NewsOne, "Racism, Riots and Police Brutality: A Never Ending Cycle," August 10, 2011. www.newsone.com.

Daniel Okrent, "The Death—and Possible Life—of a Great City," *Time*, September 24, 2009. www.time.com.

Robert M. Press, "FOCUS: Moving Back to the Inner City," *Christian Science Monitor*, April 17, 1975.

Scott Shrake, "Ashes and Embers of the Detroit Riot," *Huffington Post*, July 23, 2007. www.huffingtonpost.com.

Richard L. Strout, "Detroit Sifts Through Riot Embers for Racial Lessons," *Christian Science Monitor*, September 11, 1967.

Websites

American Experience: Eyes on the Prize (www.pbs.org/wgbh/amex/eyesontheprize). A PBS website on the civil rights movement. The site includes primary sources, videos, profiles, essays about the movement, newspaper excerpts, and many other resources.

The Detroit Riots of 1967 (www.67riots.rutgers.edu). A website maintained by Rutgers University, this site includes a narrative of events, videotaped interviews with witnesses, maps, and a bibliography.

News Photo Gallery—July 1967: Detroit Erupts (http://apps.detroitnews.com/apps/multimedia/gallery.php?id=3613). An archive of more than fifty photos with informational captions from the Detroit riots, maintained by the *Detroit News*.

INDEX